Charles Herbert Thurber

In and Out of Ithaca

A description of the village, the surrounding scenery and Cornell

University

Charles Herbert Thurber

In and Out of Ithaca
A description of the village, the surrounding scenery and Cornell University

ISBN/EAN: 9783337427412

Printed in Europe, USA, Canada, Australia, Japan

Cover: Foto ©Andreas Hilbeck / pixelio.de

More available books at **www.hansebooks.com**

IN AND OUT OF ITHACA.

A DESCRIPTION OF THE VILLAGE, THE SURROUNDING SCENERY,
AND CORNELL UNIVERSITY,

BY

C. H. THURBER.

ILLUSTRATED.

ITHACA, N. Y.
ANDRUS & CHURCH.
1887.

THE pages that follow have been prepared in the belief that it would be a source of gratification to many to be able to procure in convenient form a description of the village of Ithaca, with the rare and interesting scenery surrounding it, and also some comprehensive account of Cornell University. The facts here brought together it is hoped may be of service.

If the reader finds the first chapter on the geology of the region, interesting, his thanks, with mine, are due to Mr. G. K. Gilbert, of the Geological Survey, who has kindly given the writer some of the results of his own studies in this region. Chapters XXIV to XXVII inclusive, and the greater part of Chapter XXVIII, were written entirely by Mr. Geo. M. Marshall.

C. H. T.

CONTENTS.

ILLUSTRATIONS.

IN AND OUT OF ITHACA.

I.

THE books tell us that Ithaca was founded in 1789.
The rocks tell quite another story. Not in years,
but in aeons do they record the flight of time since our
foundations were laid. Curious and interesting is the
tale, not yet quite reclaimed from the realm of primeval
myth, but still plain enough, so that we may keep the
thread of the strange story. Like editors of some old
manuscript or translators of some ancient classic, we
will allow ourselves to supply a word here and there,
which perhaps the scientists are not quite ready to put
in, but which is needed to complete the sense, and then
the history will run as follows :—

Long ago these heaps of Chemung shale were laid
down under the water, and now and then a little spirifer
or trilobite was immortalized in the process. Then,
in the course of time, when the water went down or the
land came up—no matter now which—a great plateau
was formed through the centre of the State. Through
it ran tortuous and winding streams, as streams are
wont to be, taking off the drainage of the country northward, and having each its own little valley running in
a general way north and south. Then over this fair

scene broke the horror of the glacial epoch. Ice to an
extent which the imagination even cannot compass,
covered the land reaching down to what in distant future ages was to be the State of Pennsylvania. It filled
all these little valleys, and as it moved slowly, majesti-
cally and mercilessly over the country, it ground off
sharp corners into rounded curves, it scratched out little
irregularities completely, and in places where it stayed
longest it dug out the valley to a greater depth. The
ice gradually moved off to the north, dropping its debris
from its receding edges, and this moraine matter is now
plainly visible on the Spencer divide. It yielded a little
on the south, but the great glacial mass, like a huge
dam, still shut off the outlets of the valleys in the
north. Then in that valley which in ages to come was
to be filled by Cayuga Lake, began the action which
has resulted in the curious glens and gorges that make
our Ithaca so enchanting and bewildering a place.

As the ice receded the space it left behind was occupied by a lake, shut in at the north by the ice-dam.
The old water-courses were broken up. The little
streams poured into the lake here and there, wherever
it happened it seems, and rapidly wore away the soft
rock where they chose their channels. The debris from
this cutting process was deposited just under water at
the mouths of the streams, forming deltas. By and by
the ice-dam to the north gave way a little, and the level
of the lake was consequently lowered. These deltas
then became little terraces, and the streams cut deeper
and took down more debris to form other deltas below.

Then the ice-dam yielded a little more ; and so the process was repeated, until finally the lake reached its present level, the ice all having passed away. The successive deltas that the many streams had formed, as the lake lowered its level, now became terraces up the sides of the various ravines.*

So we see that all these ravines were given their curious and fantastic shaping, as the result of the great ice flow, which not only straightened out and improved the narrow and tortuous channel of some primeval creek to be the fit bed of our beautiful Cayuga Lake, but also in its tardy departure formed a great ice-locked lake, into which the young and inexperienced streams poured their contributions, cutting down the rock as the level of the ice-lake fell.

Such is the true story of all ·the streams, save alone Six Mile Creek, that lend their varied charms to make the setting of Ithaca so royal in its beauty. Six Mile is likely more nearly as it was in the days before the ice came over the world. There are many details of the story about which we should like to ask just one or two questions, as for example, whether the height of the various falls corresponds with successive breaks in the

---

* This terrace formation is plainly shown on the sides of the Fall Creek ravine. Professor Comstock's house stands on one terrace, the next lower one is occupied by the Sibley Building and Physical Laboratory ; the next by the McGraw-Fiske House ; the next by the mills, while the great gravel bank at the foot of the ravine is a very good example of the way in which these terraces were formed. The process may be seen going on at present, noticeably at Taughannock, where the stream is building out a great peninsula.

ice-dam and consequent lowering in the level of the ice-lake. The fact that all the lowest falls in the various ravines make the greatest leaps would seem to give an answer to our question, as decided as it is interesting. However, we may not cross-question too closely as yet, but may rest assured that we have the main facts of the story in our possession.

As we stand on one of our hills, this story will help us to understand and interpret the landscape that is presented to our view. The long sweep and graceful curves of the lake valley, and the smoothly sloping hills, save where they are serrated by the terrace-teeth in the mouth of some deep ravine, were ground out by the ice. The glacier-artist wrought our landscape. Standing by the side of some one of the deep channels cut by a fretful stream, the thought of the vast period of time during which the stream must have been at work to accomplish what it has, often comes forcibly to the mind. Yet compared to the ages that passed over valley and hills, ere the stream began its work, what it has accomplished seems like the trifling of an idle summer hour.

II.

Ithaca was not settled until George Washington became President. The certainty of some stable government, and adequate protection against their lurking foes the Indians, encouraged the colonists to push out into new regions ; and so in the very month in which Washington assumed office for the first time, April, 1789, three men, Jacob Yaple, Isaac Dumond and Peter Hinepaw, took up four hundred acres of land bounded on the west by the line of what is now Tioga street. They planted some corn on the flat, and Yaple left his younger brother to look after it, while the rest of the party went back after the good Dutch women and children. The three families, numbering some twenty souls all told, came back in September, and put up log cabins, Hinepaw on the north side of Cascadilla Creek, near the present location of Williams' Mill, the other two on East State Street, where now stands the residence of the late Adam S. Cowdry. But in 1793 these three families had the misfortune to lose their land, which passed into the possession of Simeon Dewitt. He laid out the Village of Ithaca, and encouraged settlement by the liberal terms offered to settlers. By 1798 there were half a dozen houses. In 1806 the number of buildings had increased to twelve, six or seven of which were frame. A Mr. Vrooman kept a hotel on the spot where

the Tompkins House now stands, calling it the " Ithaca
Hotel." It was from this fact that the place came to
be generally known by the name of Ithaca, although
Mr. DeWitt had bestowed that name upon it some years
previously. The village had before that been common-
ly called " The Flats," " The City," or " Sodom." In
1810 Mr. DeWitt wrote from Albany : " The place to
which I purpose to go when I have no business here, is
a village of at least thirty houses. * * * If I
should live twenty years longer, I am confident that I
should see Ithaca as important a place as Utica is
now " ; and in a letter from Ithaca, dated the same
year, he says, " I find this village considerably increased since I was here before. I have counted thirty-
eight dwelling houses, among which are, one very large,
elegant three-story house for a hotel, and five of two
stories ; the rest of one story, all generally neat frame
buildings. Besides these, there are a school-house, and
buildings for merchants' stores, and shops for carpen-
ters, cabinet-makers, blacksmiths, coopers, tanners :
and we have besides, shoe-makers, tailors, two lawyers,
one doctor, watch-cleaner, turner, miller, hatter, etc."
With all this apparent prosperity, however, there were
only two or three marriageable young ladies, and some
forty eligible young men.

So favorably started with a name and a tavern,
Ithaca steadily grew and prospered. The turnpike to
Owego, completed about 1808, and that to Geneva, completed about 1811, gave increased shipping facilities, and
the demand for Cayuga plaster, caused by the war of

1812, the supply from Nova Scotia having been shut off on account of the war, gave an impulse to commercial enterprise. In 1820 the population numbered 859. The same year the keel of the Enterprise, the first steamer built on the lake was laid, and the boat was launched May 4th, 1821. The boat connected with the Newburgh stages, making the most direct route from New York to Buffalo, the entire journey occupying only three days. The Erie Canal, completed in 1825, gave direct communication with the Atlantic seaboard. In 1834 the Ithaca and Owego railroad was completed. The old style strap rail was used throughout, and the road ascended the hill from Ithaca by two inclined planes, up the steeper of which the cars were drawn by means of a huge windlass worked by horse power. Bright anticipations of the future were, of course, raised by all these increased facilities, and Ithaca, like most nascent cities, went through its era of speculation. It was destined, however, to be prosperous, but not great as a commercial centre, and it gradually settled down to a steady growth. In 1845 the population was about 4,000, in 1860 about 7,000, and now it is nearly 12,000.

But from all this let us turn to our Ithaca, as we know it to-day, as it is loved by its citizens and admired by all comers.

III.

THE SUPERSTRUCTURE—ITHACA OF TO-DAY.

Nobly and beautifully situated, the lake stretching out its silver beauty before her, the hills rising about her to form a terraced amphitheatre, Ithaca is to-day fast realizing all that is meant by the term, a University town. Pictures of Oxford and Cambridge, of the University towns of Germany, rise before the mind in comparison with which, however, Ithaca suffers not at all. Youngest of her sisters, it is true, not yet so fully developed in all ways, but quietly and rapidly growing into her place.

The view from South Hill, coming in on the Delaware, Lackawanna and Western Railroad, the old Ithaca and Owego road, is on the whole the most comprehensive and satisfactory.* On the east and west the lake valley rises to the level of the old plateau in graceful curves, intersected here and there by some one of the numerous ravines. On East Hill the buildings of the Cornell University stand out in bold relief, Cascadilla Place in the foreground, half hidden by foliage.† To the north the placid waters of Cayuga flow out to meet the horizon, Crowbar Point, six miles down the lake, seeming to cut it off, and the water then reappearing far in the

---

* See Frontispiece.

† These buildings do not appear in the Frontispiece. See View of the Campus.

distance beyond. Right below us rise the roofs and
spires of the city itself, the Cornell Library Building,
and the new High School Building being conspicuous
among surrounding edifices. Just at the base of West
Hill runs the sluggish Inlet ; on its bank are the great ele-
vators, further to the north the steamboat landing and
the dingy coal docks. Near the base of the East Hill,
witching Willow Avenue leads the now quiet Cascadilla
to the Lake. Such is the Forest City as seen in the
whole, nestling among its hills, guarded by its sylvan
deities.

But from the hill let us come nearer, and visit those
places that we should know about, and learn how they
came to be.

IV.

THE CORNELL LIBRARY.

Ithaca early started out as a literary place. As early as in 1806, three hundred dollars worth of books were purchased to constitute a public library. Few, if any, additions were ever made to this collection, and about 1835 the books were divided up among the members of the Minerva Society, who had acquired the title to the library. The library disappeared in the way such libraries do, the various persons who had books in their possession keeping those they had, and getting as many more as they could.

In 1862, Ezra Cornell, having acquired a large fortune in building up the telegraph system of the country, came to the decision that he would be his own executor in making that fortune a blessing to other men. He decided to found a free public library. His first intention was to devote $20,000 to the purchase of a lot and the erection of a building, but on consultation with his friends, this original purpose was greatly modified, and he finally decided to start the library as it ought to be started, let the cost be what it might. With clear business foresight he recognized the fact that to ensure the permanence and prosperity of the Library it must be made self-sustaining. In accordance with this view, the present library building was erected, and dedicated with impressive ceremonies, on the the 20th of December, 1866, having cost, with the books in the library at the time of dedication, $65,676.50.

The building stands on the corner of Seneca and Tioga Streets. It is a handsome brick structure, three stories high above a finished basement. The first floor is at present occupied by the rooms of the First National Bank, the Cornell Free Reading Room, and business offices. The second floor contains the rooms for the Library, and a large hall, capable of seating over eight hundred persons. The third floor contains two large rooms over the hall, and a suit of living rooms for the janitor. The library room is thirty feet wide, fifty feet long, and twenty-four feet high, well lighted and fireproof. The space for books is divided into two tiers of alcoves, each tier containing ten alcoves, and each pair of alcoves being finished in a different native wood. The capacity of the room is about 30,000 volumes. It at present contains about 12,000. The income from the rent of the business offices and the hall has proved sufficient not only for the maintenance of the Library, but also for a steady addition to the volumes on its shelves.

The Library is controlled by the Cornell Library Association, incorporated in 1864, according to Mr. Cornell's own ideas. The Board of Trustees consists of the eldest male descendant of Ezra Cornell, the pastors of the Presbyterian, First and Second Methodist, Congregational, Episcopal, First Baptist, and Catholic churches, the principal of the Academy, the Principal of the District Schools, the Chairman of the Board of Supervisors, the President of the village, the Chief Engineer of the Fire Department, and six others. The Librarian of the Library is *ex officio*, a trustee of Cornell University.

V.

OTHER PUBLIC BUILDINGS.

On Cayuga Street, between Seneca and Buffalo, stands a graceful brick edifice that serves the village of Ithaca as High School. Ornamental in its outlines, convenient in location, and furnished in accordance with the best modern scientific ideas on education, it is an honor to the Forest City.

The corner-stone of the building was laid Sept. 2d, 1884, with imposing Masonic ceremonies. Sept. 7th, 1885, the dedicatory services were held in the building. The High School stands on the site of the old Ithaca Academy, the corporation of this institution having made over its property to the village of Ithaca in 1884. The material of the building is pressed brick, ornamented with terra cotta work. The first floor contains the rooms of the Grammar School, rooms for the Board of Education and the Superintendent, and cloak rooms. The second story contains a study hall fifty-two by sixty-five feet, a physical laboratory, four recitation rooms and the Principal's office. The entire cost of the completed building was $55,549.18. The building is furnished throughout with school furniture of the most approved construction, and supplied with every appliance to promote the good health of the pupils. The building is a noble structure, and in its completeness and efficiency well represents the public school system of Ithaca.

ITHACA.
HIGH SCHOOL BUILDING.

Aside from the High School, the public buildings of note are the Court House on DeWitt Park, and the building for the police station and the fire department, on the corner of Seneca and Tioga Streets. It can hardly be said that either of these buildings possess such architectural beauty as to attract a very careful inspection.

VI.

THE CHURCHES.

The first religious denomination to be represented by an organized church in the settlement of Ithaca was the Presbyterian. The First Presbyterian church of Ithaca was organized in 1804, with a membership of seven persons. The Rev. G. Mandeville was the first pastor, and continued to preach here and at Trumansburg on alternate Sundays for twelve years, when he became discouraged, and gave up, so little spiritual activity was manifested by the settlers. In 1816 Dr. Wisner began his labors by excommunicating six of the twenty members ; and his zeal and earnestness were rewarded by the rapid growth of the society until in 1820 it numbered one hundred and thirteen members. At that time horse racing and intemperance were not held by public opinion to be at all incompatible with the exercise of the Christian graces, and Dr. Wisner, who held a different view, had no little trouble with his congregation. The first church building was erected in 1818. In 1825 this was altered and enlarged, and so remained till 1853, when it was torn down, and the present commodious building erected. The church stands on the north-west corner of DeWitt Park, is an imposing edifice viewed from the outside, and the inside is finished with good taste and elegance. A neat brick building for lecture-room and chapel, adjoins the church on the east.

The First, or Aurora Street, Methodist church, is a handsome brick edifice, on the corner of Aurora and Mill Streets. It was erected in 1866. The society was first organized in 1794, by the Rev. John Broadhead, but soon became practically extinct. In 1817 it was revived, and in 1820 a chapel was erected on the site of the present building, and dedicated under the pastorate of the Rev. G. W. Densmore. Hitherto the villagers had been obliged to rely upon their memories to be reminded of the hour of church service, but these had doubtless been found more or less treacherous, and consequently the new chapel was equipped with a bell, the first to send its summons across Cayuga valley.

St. John's Episcopal Church was organized at a meeting held in the Methodist chapel, April 8th, 1822. In 1823 the first church edifice, a brick structure, was erected on the site of the present building. In 1844 the church was repaired and enlarged ; in 1845 a parsonage was purchased, and in 1860 the old church was torn down, and the present substantial edifice on the corner of Buffalo and Cayuga Streets, was erected in its stead. St. Paul's Episcopal church was organized in 1874, and holds services in the University Chapel.

The First Baptist Church of Ithaca, now known as the Park Baptist Church, occupies a commodious and tasteful brick building on the east side of DeWitt Park. The society was first organized in Danby village as the Danby Baptist Church, but for purposes of convenience was removed to Ithaca in 1826, taking its present name. The first church building was erected in 1830–31, and the present building in 1854.

The First Congregational Church was organized in
1830, by the Rev. John H. Schemerhorn, as the Re-
formed Protestant Dutch Church, and a building was
erected in 1830-31. In 1872 the organization was
changed to a Congregational Society, and in 1883-4 the
present handsome edifice on the corner of Seneca and
Geneva Streets was erected. Beautiful, but not especially imposing, viewed from the exterior, the church
from the interior is a model of taste, comfort and convenience.

The Second Methodist Church occupies a large brick
edifice on the corner of State and Albany Streets. The
society was organized from the First Church in 1851 ;
and first erected a frame structure on the corner of
Seneca and Plain Streets. The society was then known
as the Seneca Street M. E. Church. In 1878 the present church building was erected, and the church has
since been known as the State Street Church.

The First Unitarian Society of Ithaca was the outgrowth of a series of meetings which began in the
Town Hall on the 15th of October, 1865. The Rev.
Samuel J. May, notable in anti-slavery history, officia-
ted at this meeting, and was prominently interested in
the movement which followed. In 1868 articles of association were adopted, and the name of the society
changed to the Church of Christian Unity. The society
at present occupies a neat frame edifice on Buffalo Street
near Aurora, which was erected in 1873.

The first Catholic settlers came to Ithaca about 1830,
and a church was organized in 1834, and called the

Church of the Immaculate Conception. The first building was erected in 1851, and the present church, on the corner of Seneca and Geneva Streets, in 1860.

The Tabernacle Baptist Church, organized in 1870, occupies a small house of worship on Railroad Avenue. At present the foundations are laid for a new church edifice adjoining the one now occupied.

The Free Methodist Society, organized in 1871, occupies a building on North Tioga Street.

The African M. E. Zion Church was organized in 1833, and has long occupied a modest edifice on Wheat Street.

The Wesleyan (colored) M. E. Church, was organized from the Zion Church in 1851, and occupies a building on North Albany Street.

VII.

"TRADE—THE CALM HEALTH OF NATIONS."

In fine stores and well-conducted business enterprises of various sorts Ithaca has never been deficient. But certain products of the Forest City are unique in their interest, and have borne her name into every quarter of the civilized world, and some quarters even of the uncivilized. Chief of these is the Ithaca Calendar Clock. Where has your early lot in life been cast, that you have not heard of or seen an Ithaca Calendar Clock? Nothing has given the clock-making profession so much fame as this highest product of its skill, and the manufacture of the Ithaca calendar is the aristocracy of clockmaking. The first really successful patent for a perpetual clock calendar, was obtained by Mr. Horton, of Ithaca, in 1865 ; and this, improved and modified, is the one now owned by the Ithaca Calendar Clock Co. As now made it indicates perpetually the day of the month, the month of the year, and the day of the week. The works on Adams Street, in the northern part of the city, contain much interesting special machinery of exceedingly ingenious construction.

In the same building is the factory of the Autophone Company, which manufactures the autophone, one of the most ingenious of the many automatic musical instruments that are so peculiar a product of the latter half of the nineteenth century.

Not far from the clock factory, and nearer the Inlet, are the Ithaca Glass Works. The plant is one of the largest and best arranged in the country, and produces some 9,000 boxes of white crystal sheet glass monthly. One of the youngest of Ithaca's larger industries, it is one of the most interesting, as it is one of the most promising.

If we can consider the press as a business enterprise, and certainly the business side of journalism is by no means its least important side, there is no better place than this in which to speak of the newspapers that supply the Forest City with its daily mental food.

The journalistic traditions of the past centre around the *Ithaca Journal.* The *Journal* is the lineal descendant of the *Seneca Republican,* which first came from the press in 1815, as a twelve by fourteen inch paper, published by Johnathan Ingersoll. In 1816 the name was changed to the *Ithaca Journal.* The name changed, however, almost as often as the proprietors, and that was with rather regular frequency, until in 1841 the paper came into the control of John H. Selkreg, who revived the old name, by which it has since been known. Rivals sprang up, only to be absorbed. In 1872, after many unsuccessful attempts by other parties to make a daily live, the *Daily Journal* was started, and has met with a steady and satisfactory support. The paper is now controlled by the Ithaca Journal Association. Originally Democratic in politics, the *Journal* became republican when the slavery question became a vital issue, and has since remained so.

The *Ithaca Democrat* traces its lineage to the *Ithaca Chronicle*, established in 1820 by D. D. Spencer. The *Chronicle*, like the *Journal*, experienced many vicissitudes of ownership and name, but finally settled down to be called the *Democrat* in 1867. In 1884, the *Daily Democrat* made its appearance, and was successful in its object of offering democratic opposition to the republican influence of the *Daily Journal*. It was discontinued shortly after the elections.

Rumsey's Companion, established at Dryden in 1856, was the progenitor of the *Weekly Ithacan*. After many vicissitudes the paper was removed to Ithaca in 1871. It is devoted to local interests, temperance, and greenbacks.

The *Ithaca Republican* was established as a weekly paper in 1885. It has been so successful as to warrant its advance to a tri-weekly, and though youngest of Ithaca's journals, has already taken its share of patronage and influence.

VIII.

This you say, is not all that can be said about Ithaca, but you will agree with me that not all that can be said is worth saying in a book of this character. We seek only to give those features of our village that are of most general interest, or that are unique, and so distinguish it from other villages of the same kind. As it is well known to be a prosperous place of good repute, we shall take it for granted that it will be known without our telling that there are pleasant streets, and beautiful homes, good citizens, and it may be some bad ones, city government, firemen, good ones, police, and all that goes to make such a village as Ithaca is known to be. Only to one place more must we turn our attention before tracing the growth of the noble seat of learning that crowns East Hill. That is the city where dwell the peaceful dead. On the wooded slopes of the eastern hillside, in view of the silver lake, with Cascadilla's murmurous waters whispering a lullaby, they sleep, till the water shall stop flowing, and the lullaby shall cease. In peacefulness and quiet beauty, there are few cemeteries that surpass that of the Forest City.

IX.

INTRODUCTORY.

Cornell University was first opened to receive students in October, 1868. At that time there were only two buildings, neither of which was completed. Professors and students propped up the doors to their rooms when they retired at night, because the hinges and the locks had not yet been put on, and the sound of Greek recitations and the blows of the hammer resounded from adjoining rooms. There were no walks, the ground was rough and uneven, and the corn field still held its place on the summit of the hill. Everything was lacking for a great University, except great men, and grand ideas. To-day the alumni of this institution number more than a thousand, scattered over this land and almost all others. Ten stately buildings of brick and stone, surrounded by a smooth and well graded campus, have supplanted the cornfield. Rows of flourishing elms interlace their branches over pleasant walks and winding drives. Nearly seven hundred students throng its halls, and are taught in all branches of human learning. Among the few institutions that make American scholarship respected everywhere, it occupies a foremost place. Foreign scholars speak of it with respect, and esteem it an honor to lecture in its halls. And it has

CORNELL UNIVERSITY.

View of Campus and Buildings from Sage College—Cayuga Lake in the distance.

exercised an influence upon higher education in America that words cannot express. The history of education shows no parallel to the growth and development of this University. What are the secrets of this growth?

We shall find an adequate explanation for the success of Cornell University in the men who have built it, and in the foundations upon which they built. Ezra Cornell's heart and hand, and Andrew D. White's heart and brain, are wrought into its very texture. It was not alone Ezra Cornell's gift of money, and devotion to the care of the University funds that constituted his inestimable service in its advancement, but it was even more the broad and liberal foundations upon which he would have it built. Andrew D. White lent to the work a wide experience in other institutions of learning, a breadth and catholicity of culture seldom equalled, great liberality of opinion and unusual administrative talent. During the life-time of Mr. Cornell he was nobly assisted by such men as John McGraw, Hiram Sibley and Henry W. Sage, and after his death the Trustees proved themselves worthy to carry on the great undertaking. No institution ever encountered severer opposition, none ever went through darker trials, but she has conquered opposition and difficulties, and is to-day richer, stronger and more prosperous than ever before.

X.

HISTORY.

The history of Cornell University begins with the so-called Morrill Grant of 1862. In that year, the Hon. Justin S. Morrill, United States Senator from Vermont, introduced into Congress, and secured the passage of a bill granting to each State thirty thousand acres of the public lands for each Senator and Representative in Congress. The object of the act was plainly expressed in the words, "the endowment, support and maintenance of at least one college where the leading object shall be, without excluding other scientific and classical studies, and including military tactics, to teach such branches of learning as are related to agriculture and the mechanic arts, in such manner as the legislatures of the States may respectively prescribe, in order to promote the liberal and practical education of the industrial classes in the several pursuits and professions of life." Under this law, New York received land scrip representing 990,000 acres of land. On certain easy conditions this entire grant was, in May, 1863, transferred by the Legislature of the State of New York to the People's College at Havana, N. Y. This action had not been taken without a good deal of opposition, for the various colleges throughout the State wanted the grant divided, the State Agricultural College at Ovid pushing its claims with especial vigor.

In the legislature of 1864, Andrew D. White, of
Syracuse, N. Y., was chairman of the Senate Commit-
tee on Public Instruction. In that capacity, his attention was called to a bill for incorporating a public library in Ithaca, to which Mr. Cornell proposed to give
$100,000. This led to the beginning of a friendship
that lasted until the death of Mr. Cornell in 1874, and
which was to be fruitful of the most important results
to the cause of higher education.

It had by this time become evident that the People's
College would not be able to meet the conditions on
which the land grant had been made over to it, and
that the grant would consequently revert to the State.
The twenty colleges of the State were anxious that the
sum should be divided among them. As the scrip was
then worth not more than $600,000 all told, this would
have given to each some $30,000, a meagre endowment
for a single professorship. Mr. Cornell, being a Trustee
of the State Agricultural College at Ovid, favored the
division of the grant into two parts, giving one to the
People's College, and one to the Agricultural College.
From the first, Mr. White steadily opposed any division
whatever. It seemed to him a providential opportunity for the establishment of a great university in the
centre of the State of New York, which should be
built upon better principles than had hitherto prevailed,
and should make the best provisions for modern scientific and technical instruction. Such an institution had
long been in his mind.*

---

* At the inauguration of President White in 1868, Mr. Geo.
William Curtis used these words : " My friends, it is now just

He had once offered to add half his own private fortune to the endowment of such a University, and the way now seemed open for realizing his long cherished wish.

The legislature being unable to come to an agreement upon any one of the various plans before it for disposing of the land scrip, adjourned without taking action. During the ensuing summer, Mr. Cornell, after a vain effort had been made to induce Mr. White to acquiesce in a compromise, by which half the sum should go to the Agricultural College, and half remain where it was with the People's College, finally became fully converted to Mr. White's ideas. He accordingly came forward and offered, provided the State would establish an en-

---

about ten years since I was in the city of Ann Arbor, Michigan, the seat of the University of Michigan. . . . I was in that city, and I sat at night talking with my friend, a New York scholar, Professor of History in that institution, and one of the men who have given that institution its great place in this country. There, in the warmth and confidence of his friendship, he unfolded to me his idea of the great work that should be done in the great State of New York. 'Surely,' he said, 'in the greatest State there should be the greatest of Universities; in central New York there should arise a University which by the amplitude of its endowment, and by the whole scope of its intended sphere, by the character of the studies in the whole scope of its curriculum, should satisfy the wants of the hour.' 'More than that,' he said, 'it should begin at the beginning. It should take hold of the chief interest of the country, which is agriculture; then it should rise—step by step—grade by grade—until it fulfilled the highest ideal of what a University should be.' Until the hour was late this young scholar dreamed aloud to me these dreams, and at the close, at our parting, our consolation was, that we lived in a country that was open to every generous idea, and that his dream one day might be realized, was still a possibility."

tirely new institution and locate it at Ithaca, to endow
the same with the sum of $500,000. A bill to establish
Cornell University, and to appropriate to it the income
from the sale of the public lands granted to the State by
the act of 1862, was therefore introduced into the next
session of the Senate by Mr. White. Mr. White, Mr.
Cornell, and Mr. Folger, late Secretary of the Treasury,
and then a State Senator, drew the bill with great care.

The strife that followed was prolonged and bitter.
Every artifice of political trickery and wire-pulling pol-
iticians was brought to bear against its passage. The
smaller colleges cried for their share. Compromise was
proposed to Mr. Cornell, but he rejected the idea with
scorn. He would let the legislature put what it pleased
in the bill, and he would then accept or reject its provisions, but he would not buy the silence of his oppo-
nents. As the result of this long struggle, the bill
was passed by the Senate, with an amendment providing
that the scrip should remain with the People's College,
in case it fulfilled the conditions of its grant within
three years ; and it came out of the Assembly with
an absurd amendment requiring Mr. Cornell to give
$25,000 to endow a chair of Agricultural Chemisty in
Genesee College, a small Methodist institution at Lima,
N. Y., before the representatives of the people would
permit him to give $500,000 to the people whom they
represented. The bill thus amended, became a law on
the 27th of April, 1865.

The People's College again failed to comply with the
conditions for making the grant its own, and conse-

quently the entire amount of the land scrip came into
the full possession of Cornell University. Mr. Cornell
paid Genesee College the $25,000 required by the act,
executed his bond for $500,000 bearing seven per cent.
interest, in favor of the University, and in addition gave
two hundred and thirty acres of land as a site for the
University and a University farm.

But this was by no means all. The State of New
York not having any public land within its own borders, could not locate the scrip, and was therefore
obliged to sell it at the market price. Owing to the
great amount of the scrip thrown upon the market, the
price was rapidly forced down. An average price of
about sixty cents an acre was all that could have been
derived from the sale of the lands, and the endowment
from this source, therefore, in case the scrip had been
sold, would have amounted to little more than $600,000.
There was only one way in which a larger sum could
be realized. The State could sell the scrip to the
Trustees, who could themselves locate the land for the
State. An act was accordingly passed, the substance of
which was, that the State offered to sell the land to the
Trustees at thirty cents per acre, and if this offer was
not accepted by the Trustees, offered to sell the scrip
to any person or persons who would give security that
the profits arising from the location and sale of the
lands would be turned over to the State, to be added to
the endowment of the University. The Trustees of the
University were not in a condition to avail themselves
of the provisions of the act, and accordingly Mr. Cor-

nell assumed the responsibility of purchasing and locating the scrip at his own expense. In a letter to the Comptroller, dated June 9th, 1866, Mr. Cornell says:

"I shall most cheerfully accept your views so far as to consent to place the entire profits to be derived from the sale of lands to be located with the College Land Scrip in the treasury of the State, if the State will receive the money as a separate fund from that which may be derived from the sale of the scrip, and will keep it permanently invested, and appropriate the proceeds from the income thereof annually to the Cornell University, subject to the direction of the Trustees thereof, for the general purposes of the said institution, and not to hold it subject to the restrictions which the act of Congress places upon the funds derived from the sale of the College Land Scrip, or as a donation from the government of the United States, but as a donation from Ezra Cornell to the Cornell University."

This letter is of great importance in the history of the University, especially in view of recent criticisms upon the broadening of the courses of study beyond those branches plainly indicated in the original act of Congress. The State accepted Mr. Cornell's proposition, and now the greater part of the income of the University arises from the Cornell Endowment fund, which is expressly stated not to be subject to the restrictions of the act of Congress. This clearly gives the Trustees the right to use the income arising from this fund in expanding the scope of the University in any way their judgment may dictate.

Of Mr. Cornell and his labors in connection with locating this land, the Hon. Henry W. Sage, in his address at the inauguration of President Adams, spoke as follows : "His first gift was half a million dollars to secure to Cornell the Land Grant from the United States to this State : after that in various ways, half as much more ; and last and greatest, his undertaking with the State to carry for twenty years at his own cost five hundred thousand acres of land for which the scrip was worth but $300,000, to sell the same, and return the net proceeds to the treasury of the State for the benefit of Cornell University. The sum thus to be procured from the lands he estimated at more than $2,000,000.

He carried his burden eight years, expending for that purpose over $500,000 of his own cash ; but during all that time the total sales of land paid but a fraction of his expenses for carrying. Meantime the misfortune of unavailable investments and failing health rendered him unable longer to carry the lands, and on his death-bed he said in substance to the Trustees : 'I can no longer do this work ; take it and do it for me, but' (with the old-time invincible courage and faith,) 'don't fear the result, it will be all I ever expected.' And it has been. The Trustees assumed his burden, and with loving hearts and willing hands, saving every farthing for its destined work, without the cost of a dollar for their administration, have already placed in the treasury of the University much more than the largest sum estimated by him, and the final outcome will be double that sum."

It was for this work that Mr. Cornell was assailed as a " thief " and a " land-grabber," and his declining years embittered by the most unjust and unwarranted assaults in many of the papers of the State.

Such is the history of Cornell's magnificent endowment. To the sum thus secured very important additions have been made by the Hon. Henry W. Sage, the founder of Sage College, the Hon. Hiram Sibley, founder of Sibley College, John McGraw, who gave the McGraw Building, Ex-President White, whose gifts to the University in money have exceeded $100,000, and Mrs. Jennie McGraw-Fiske, who gave the University Chime, and by her will made the University Library the residuary legatee of her large estate, amounting to nearly a million of dollars.*

---

*This will is now being contested in the courts. The progress of the suit thus far has been altogether favorable to the University.

XI.

ORGANIZATION AND INFORMING IDEAS.

Under the new charter a Board of Trustees was appointed, and Mr. White was asked to draw up a plan of organization. On the twenty-first of October, 1866, he presented his plan to the Board. As a result, on the twenty-fourth of October, 1866, Mr. White was unanimously chosen President of Cornell University, a position which he continued to hold for twenty years. He was unwilling at first to accept the position, as he had important business interests in Syracuse, and had moreover, just been elected Director of the Art School, and Lecturer on the History of Art, at Yale College.

He yielded, however, to his desire to see the new institution successfully started, and to the earnest persuasions of Mr. Cornell, and accepted the position, his intention being to hold it for a brief time only, in order to aid in the organization of the institution and in the selection of his successor. Complying with the request of Mr. Cornell and the Trustees, he shortly after went to Europe, and spent some time in investigating the school systems of England, France and Germany, having reference more especially to technical and agricultural education. He had the good fortune while abroad to secure Professor Goldwin Smith, of the University of Oxford, for the chair of English History, and Dr. James Law, of London College, for the chair of Veterinary Science.

The terms of the charter required the University to be opened for the registration of students in 1868. On Wednesday, Oct. 7th of that year, Cornell University was formally opened. The material condition in which that date found the institution has already been described. Nevertheless twenty resident, and six non-resident professors had been appointed, while over three hundred students had passed their entrance examinations.

Of those ideas which from the very outset have distinguished Cornell from every other great institution of learning in the country, the first embodiment is found in the charter of the University. That instrument provides that the University shall teach such branches of learning as are related to agriculture and the mechanic arts, including military science and tactics, together with such other branches of knowledge as the Trustees may deem useful and proper. Cornell, in other words, puts all truth on a level, and gives, and has always given, the scientific or technical student precisely the same standing in her halls and on her campus, as the student in literature and the classics. That charter further provided that persons of every religious denomination or of no religious denomination shall be equally eligible to all offices and appointments ; and that a free scholarship shall be given yearly in each assembly district to the successful competitor in an open examination.

Mr. Cornell simply and plainly indicated his own noble purpose in founding the University in that sentence which has become classic, " I would found an institution where any person can find instruction in any study."

But the hand after all, that had most to do with shaping
the ideas that were to take form in the University, was
the same hand whose ceaseless devotion to its interests
has built these ideas into brick and stone, and the lives
of thousands of students, the hand of Andrew D.
White. What was his conception of the University?
This is nowhere better expressed than in the inaugu-
ral address of President Adams, his successor in the
Presidency of Cornell University, and life-long friend :
"What was that idea? It was a very confident belief that higher education could never meet the require-
ments of this century, unless it put itself, far more
perfectly than had hitherto been done, into accord with
the feeling, the inspirations, the needs, and the demands
of the present civilization. The incoming of political
equality and the revolution of the inventions had resulted in what may be called the industrial age, and
had brought new demands that could not be ignored.
These changes, amounting to nothing less than complete
transformation of the conditions of society, must be
recognized and accepted. The new power was with the
masses of the people ; and here, as never before, an
effort needed to be made to plant university instruction
upon the necessities, the feelings, and the aspirations of
the whole people. Here, as never before, education
was to be made an outgrowth of these needs and aspirations. Here the belief was held that to limit higher
education to the classical methods of the fathers would
be to limit it to what had come to be regarded as a choice
and delicate plant that was outside the thoughts of nine-

tenths of the whole population, and that was tending, as statistics showed, to be regarded more and more exotic, no longer thought essential even by some of the learned professions. It took the ground that the university of the Nineteenth Century could be fully developed only by recognizing the needs and the methods of the Nineteenth Century, and that, while classical and literary studies were not to be neglected, but on the contrary were to be continued and developed as never before, they could no longer lay claim to be the whole field and scope of higher education. In short, all through the discussion of these formative days of Cornell University the idea ran like a thread of light that the new university must rest upon a broader foundation, must awaken the instincts of classes that had long stood aloof, must recognize the necessities not only of all the professions, but of all the industrial vocations, and that when this was done fully and honestly and boldly, the classes that had hitherto stood indifferent to the universities, or stood sullenly apart from them, would rally to their support, and would not only tolerate, but would rejoice in the development even of those studies which they regarded as most unpractical.''

The principles of the democracy of truth, and the educating influences of freedom lay at the bottom of the organization of Cornell University; and it is on these principles that her unparalleled development, materially and intellectually has taken place.

The Register of the University has the following statement as to the religious position of Cornell : ''The

University, established by a government which recognizes no distinction of religious belief, seeks neither to promote any creed, nor to exclude any." This entirely proper and just attitude of the University, has from the time of its establishment almost to the present, been the basis for the most unwarranted and unjustifiable attacks. "Godless," and "atheistic," "the hot-bed of infidelity," are some of the milder terms that have been applied to it. These attacks have come in the main from people who are unable to understand and properly interpret the real attitude of the University. As a matter of fact, there is quite as much religious earnestness among students of Cornell as there is at most other colleges, and it may well be questioned whether there is not more genuine, intelligent faith. Mr. Dean Sage gave the University $30,000 to endow the Sage Chapel pulpit, and on this endowment some forty sermons are preached every year by leaders of Christian thought of every denomination. No such course of sermons is presented anywhere else in this country, and it may be doubted whether their equal is to be found in the world. The influence of these discourses upon the thoughtful student body can hardly be over-estimated. Moreover, there is a University Christian Association, to which members of all churches are eligible, and the organization now has a membership of about one hundred and eighty, and is doing an active work in the University.

" Another idea that was embedded in the foundations of this University, was the co-equal education of women.

At the very first the Founder and the President both
put themselves distinctly before the public as favoring
the admission of women to all the privileges of the University, as soon as the needed building for their accom-
modation could be provided. The friends of the meas-
ure had not long to wait, thanks to the appreciative
generosity of one of the board of Trustees. Sage College was built and endowed as the fruit of this purpose ;
and the Trustees in accepting the gift, put upon lasting
record the two-fold declaration inscribed on the corner-
stone : ' This building with its Endowment is the Gift
of Henry W. Sage ;'* and 'In return for this Gift, the
Cornell University is pledged to provide and forever
maintain facilities for the education of Women, as
broadly as for Men.' ''

Such is the history of the foundation of Cornell University. Broad and deep were those foundations laid.
What has been the superstructure ?

* The building cost $150,000, and the endowment was $100,-
000.

XII.

DESCRIPTION OF THE CAMPUS AND BUILDINGS.

GENERAL.

The buildings of Cornell University are situated upon a commanding bluff east of the village of Ithaca. The college grounds are bounded on the north by Fall Creek Gorge and on the south by the Cascadilla Ravine. The Campus extends between these, a distance of about half a mile, and the farm lies adjoining the Campus to the east, on the summit of the plateau.

An elevation of more than four hundred feet above the lake valley gives a commanding view of the lake for nearly twenty miles of its extent from all points of the Campus, while to the south the disappearance of the valley among the surrounding hills presents a view both picturesque and delightful. The universal testimony of persons who have visited many colleges is to the effect that in beauty of location Cornell surpasses all others. In spite of the large number of buildings, the extent of the Campus is such as to give the visitor an impression of roominess. The larger number of buildings are collected in a group at the northern end of the Campus, but the Cascadilla building and the Armory are located at the other end of the grounds, on opposite sides of Cascadilla ravine, and Sage College and Chapel occupy the central space. There are ample lawns, base ball grounds, drill grounds, tennis grounds and foot ball grounds, and in spite of the fact that nowhere is the sign 'Keep off the grass' visible, the turf is generally in perfect condition, in striking contrast to the ill-used appearance of the grass on many college campuses.

To reach the University grounds visitors, if in carriages, usually ascend State Street to Eddy, drive around Cascadilla building, and cross the iron bridge over the Cascadilla ravine. If on foot, the route is more often up Seneca, or Buffalo to Eddy. For purposes of description it is convenient and usual to take up the buildings and points of interest as they would present themselves to one entering the grounds in this way.

XIII.

Cascadilla Place stands on the south bank of Cascadilla Ravine. This was the first building owned by the University. It was originally started as a water-cure establishment in 1866, but was secured by the University and finished and fitted up for its uses. The cost of the building was over $72,000, of which sum the citizens of Ithaca contributed $35,000. The building is a massive structure of stone one hundred and ninety by one hundred feet, four stories high. It contains nearly two hundred rooms which are mainly occupied by professors and their families, and students. The first floor contains a large dining hall, and an immense reception room, occupying the greater part of the west front. For many years these rooms have been used very little, but the dining hall is now operated again by private parties.

At the opening of the University this building contained the Faculty room, the Registrar's office, and recitation rooms. Many of the Faculty and a large number of students had apartments in the building, and this was under strict military discipline. The students were required to wear a uniform, their movements were regulated by the bell and drum, and their ears were accustomed to the sound of the tattoo and the reveille. The basement was fitted up with kitchen, bakeries, laundry, bath-rooms etc., on the scale of a great hotel. The dining hall was filled, and the large reception room was the scene of many pleasant social gatherings, as well as of the more formal Commencement receptions. This room contains a convenient stage, and in later years has been occcasionally used for amateur dramatic performances.

Beyond Cascadilla the road runs along the brink of the ravine, while to the right the land rises in a graceful terrace to Willow Pond, which supplies water for the building. Presently the road crosses the ravine by an iron bridge. Here, when the University opened, was only a wooden foot-bridge much farther down the bank than the present structure. The latter was built in 1874 at an expense of $7000. Directly under the bridge is the Giant's Staircase, one of the prettiest of the Cascadilla cascades. The distance of the base of the fall from the roadway is one hundred feet. The view from the bridge looking down the glen and across the valley to the hill beyond is at all seasons exquisitely beautiful —"one of the glories of Ithaca,—an exquisite bit of scenery scarcely excelled even in the mountain valleys of Piedmont." An electric light now stands at the approach to the bridge, and its light thrown upon the sides of the ravine and the interlacing branches of the pines, makes a striking picture, especially in winter, when the snow-laden boughs and the ice-sheeted walls make an effect as weird as it is impressive.

Above the bridge walks are laid out on either side of the ravine. The one on the south winding along between a bright little brook on one hand and the dark gorge on the the other is known as the "Goldwin Smith Walk." A mass of shale about half way up reached by a little side path, is the "Agassiz Rock." The path crosses the stream by a rustic bridge, and returning on the other side is there known as the "Lowell Walk." Beyond the bridge the road to the Campus leads up a sharp ascent, with abrupt banks rising on either side. On the bank to the right is the chapter house of the Kappa Alpha fraternity, erected in 1886 ; on the left is the chapter house of the Psi Upsilon fraternity, completed in 1884. Both are handsome structures.

CORNELL UNIVERSITY.
ARMORY AND GYMNASIUM HALL.

XIV.

This building, situated just at the top of the hill on the right of the road, was completed in the winter of 1883–84. The main portion is of brick, one hundred and fifty feet long, sixty feet wide and fifty feet high. The Annex, joining the main hall on the south, is a two-storied wooden building, having an area of fifty-two by thirty-eight feet. The main building, with the exception of a small portion that is set apart for an office and military store-room, is used for gymnastics and military drill. Here are to be found the arms and equipments of the cadet corps, and a carefully selected lot of the most improved gymnastic apparatus and appliances for both individual and class work. The hall is heated by steam and lighted by electricity, and, it is believed, gives the largest clear space for floor room of any gymnasium in the country. The Annex contains on the lower floor the offices of the Department of Physical Culture, faculty dressing-room, general bath and dressing-rooms, lavatory, closets and general repair room. The upper floor is entirely given up to a dressing-room, which contains locker accommodations for five hundred students. The steam heating apparatus is all contained in a brick building removed some fifty feet from the other buildings. The building is surrounded by ample lawns used as drill grounds, and for various athletic exercises, although the main athletic grounds are situated in the more northern portion of the Campus. All men students, natives of America, are, unless excused for physical disability or by reason of their being obliged to support themselves by their own labor, required to drill three days a week, one hour each day, during the first and third terms of the Freshman and Sophomore years. Each student is required to provide himself with the uniform of the corps. Arms and accoutrements are furnished by the government. The drill is under the charge of an officer in the regular army who is specially detailed for this service. Every student on entering the University is carefully examined by the Professor of Physical Culture, and if found defective in bodily development is required to take special exercise suited to his needs in the gymnasium. It is open for voluntary exercise to all other students free of charge.

CORNELL UNIVERSITY.
SAGE COLLEGE.

XV.

Just beyond the Armory the avenue crosses a pretty
little ravine by a solid causeway, and then divides, one
branch continuing directly north to the main University
buildings, passing on its way a row of professors' cottages, and the other branch turning to the right and
making a circuit between a wide lawn on the left and
rows of brilliant flowers and graceful shrubs on the
right to the front of Sage College. In architectural
plan and beauty of location, this building is the hand-
somest of the University buildings, as it is the most
expensive. It was completed in 1875, and owes its
erection to the munificence of the Hon. Henry W.
Sage, who sought by this means to bring the advantages
of the highest education within the reach of women.
The building is in the Italian Gothic style, and is constructed in the form of a quadrangle. Passing up a
broad flight of stone steps the visitor finds himself in
front of the beautiful central porch. A light enclosed
balcony projects overhead, and heavy columns of
polished Quincy granite guard the entrance on either
side. The main entrance leads into a hall which runs
the entire length of the building, On the south it opens
into the general parlor, a large, handsome room, with
substantial and elegant furniture. On the north it leads
the way to the general dining room, where there are ac-

commodations for over a hundred boarders. The space on the second, third and fourth stories is occupied by suites of rooms for women students.

Just before reaching the parlor, the visitor may turn to the left and passing through a short hallway gain access to the botanical lecture room, where the lectures on botany, and many of the courses in history are delivered. The lecture room seats about three hundred. Beyond are the private rooms of the Professors of Botany, and the botanical laboratory. Passing through the laboratory the way leads into the large greenhouses connected with the building. These were erected in 1882, also by Mr. Sage, at a cost of $15,000. The collection in the conservatories embraces many rare tropical plants, including the banana, orange, and lemon, the papyrus, eucalyptus and lotus. In the winter the mass of bloom and perfume always found there makes the conservatories the favorite resort of the student.

Above the botanical lecture room, reached by a staircase in the octagonal tower on the south, is the botanical museum. Two cases on one side of the room contain the Horace Mann Herbarium presented to the University by President White. There are several thousand species, including specimens from all parts of the world. In other cases are specimens of over a thousand different kinds of wood polished and arranged to show the difference in structure ; collections of fruits, nuts, fibres and alcoholic specimens : besides a large number of Auzoux and Brendel models. The north side of the court is nearly enclosed by the gymnasium, where gymnastic exercises especially adapted to ladies are conducted by the Professor of Physical Culture. The surroundings of Sage College are beautified by beds and borders of foliage plants and brilliant flowers, and every effort is made to make life as pleasant as possible for the inmates.

XVI.

SAGE CHAPEL.

Beyond Sage College the road crosses a little glen on a bridge of solid masonry and comes presently to Sage Chapel, a handsome brick structure, in the Gothic style. The building was erected by the Hon. Henry W. Sage, at a cost of $30,000 and presented to the University. The building is constructed with a large auditorium seating about four hundred, and a small wing on the south capable of seating about one hundred. The main auditorium is noteworthy for the number of memorial windows and memorial tablets that it contains. The large memorial window over the pulpit in the eastern end was placed by the Hon. Henry W. Sage in memory of his wife. The window is divided into twelve parts, in three rows of four sections each ; the scenes in the upper and lower rows are taken from the parables of the New Testament, while the middle row is made up of allegorical figures. Another very handsome window in the south was placed by President White in memory of an infant son. A window in the north east corner was placed by the classmates and friends of Margaret Hicks in her memory. Tablets in bronze and stone line the northern wall, commemorating among others the founder, Ezra Cornell, Bayard Taylor, and Professor Hartt. In a recess under the tower is placed a large pipe organ of excellent quality, the gift of Mr. Wm. H. Sage. The high vaulted ceiling interlaced with beams, the solid walnut seats, together with the stained windows and many memorials, give the interior of the chapel, a decidedly European appearance.

On the north side of the main chapel is the Memorial Chapel, constructed in the Gothic style of the second or decorative period. It was erected, as a tablet in its northern end bears witness, to the memory of Ezra Cornell, John McGraw, and Jennie McGraw-Fiske, and was completed in 1884. Though the exterior is of brick with stone trimmings, the interior, which is finished in pure Gothic, is of Caen stone supported in vaulted arches by ribs of Ohio sandstone. On entering the chapel the eye is at once arrested by the rich memorial windows constructed by Clayton & Bell of London. They are designed not only to commemorate the connection of Mr. Cornell, Mr. McGraw, and Mrs. Jennie McGraw-Fiske with this University, but also to associate their names with the names of some of the greatest benefactors in the cause of education. The north window contains the figures of William of Wykeham, John Harvard, and Ezra Cornell ; the east window the figures of Jeanne of Navarre, Margaret of Richmond, and Jennie McGraw-Fiske ; the west window those of Elihu Yale, Sir Thomas Bodley, and John McGraw. Directly beneath the great northern window is a recumbent figure of Ezra Cornell, in white marble, of heroic size, by William W. Story, of Rome. A crypt underneath the chapel contains recesses for the remains of the founders of the University. On the exterior, allegorical figures of Munificentia and Beneficentia adorn the east and west sides respectively.

XVII.

ON THE WAY TO THE PRESIDENT'S HOUSE.

Beyond Sage Chapel the side avenue by which Sage College is reached again joins the main avenue, which then leads to the main University Buildings, the first of which is Morrill Hall. Just before the road reaches Morrill Hall another side avenue branches off to the right and runs directly east to the President's House. On the right of this avenue near the President's House stands an immense pine, beneath which is a massive carved stone seat, placed there by Professor Goldwin Smith. The seat bears the inscription "Above all nations is humanity." Up the rugged sides of the pine a tender ivy is now making its way, while a brass tablet sunk in the trunk, bears the inscription " Ivy, Class of 1886." In front of the President's House the side avenue joins East Avenue which runs parallel with the main avenue from the Armory, some distance east of the latter. On this corner stands a brown stone bearing the inscription "Ostrander Elms." The significance of this inscription is often an object of inquiry, and the following interesting explanation may not be known to all.*

"And last, not least, a gift which has always had for me a fragrance akin to that of the widow's mite

---

*From the address of the Hon. Henry W. Sage at the Inauguration of President Adams.

immortalized in Scripture. John B. Ostrander, a man
remarkable for his integrity and humility, after having
served me twenty-five years in the forests of Canada and
Michigan, returned at the age of seventy to Dryden,
his native town, to spend there his declining years.
Meeting me one day he said, 'Henry, I have been to
the University grounds and seen the work in progress
there, and feel as if I want to do something to help it
along. Now, I have no money, but I have been think-
ing ; I have some fine young elms in my woods, and I
can bring down thirty or forty and plant them there.
They will make the grounds look better, and will make
a shade for somebody after you and I are gone.' I re-
plied : 'They are just what we want, bring them and
they shall be known as the 'Ostrander Elms.' Those
are the elms on East Avenue, and a stone at each end
of the row marks the name of the donor. The shadow
of death has rested over his tomb several years, and not
long hence will rest over mine, but the elms remain,
and a hundred years hence the shadows of their graceful foliage will attest the loving gift he made us,—'will
make a shade for somebody.' "

Here, perhaps, is the place to say that the thriving
elms whose graceful boughs shade the main avenues
were given to the University by the late Dr. Fitzhugh
of Geneseo, a brother-in-law of Gerrit Smith.

The President's House was erected by President
White in 1871 at a cost of $50,000 and donated to the
University to be ever occupied by the President. It is
a large brick structure, in the Swiss Gothic style.

Standing somewhat back from the road, and half hidden by the foliage of the native forest trees that surround it, it presents a charming picture. The house contains, besides many valuable works of art, the larger part of the private library of President White, numbering some 20,000 volumes.

East Avenue extends north of the President's House till it terminates on a bluff near the bank of Fall Creek. Throughout its entire length it is lined with the residences of members of the Faculty, each residence being unique in design, and differing completely from all the others. Bordered with a broad stone walk shaded by elms, East Avenue is one of the pleasantest parts of the University grounds.

XVIII

MORRILL HALL AND WHITE HALL.

Returning again to the Main Avenue at the point where the drive branches off to the President's House, the visitor first comes to a large stone building on the left of the avenue. This is Morrill Hall. This building was the first one erected by the University, and shares with Cascadilla the honor of having accommodated the first classes. When first erected it was called, "The University." After other buildings were erected it was called South Hall. Finally it was formally named Morrill Hall in honor of the Hon. Justin S. Morrill. The material of the building is blue stone quarried on the University grounds, with trimmings of light Medina stone. The building is divided into three divisions or halls, by partitions running from roof to basement. In the south hall are the offices of the President, the Treasurer, the Dean and the Registrar, on the first floor. The upper floors are occupied by lecture rooms. In the middle hall on the left is the Faculty Room, where the meetings of the General Faculty are held. In this room are large oil portraits of Ex-President White, the Hon. Hiram Sibley, and the Hon. Justin S. Morrill. The portrait of the Hon. Henry W. Sage is soon to be added to the collection. On the right of the hall is the Agricultural museum, which also occupies the basement under the north hall. The museum contains a large collection of models of agricultural implements, as well as specimens of farm products. The remainder of this building is occupied by lecture rooms, the second and third stories of the northern hall containing the rooms of the architectural department.

The next building to the Morrill Hall is the McGraw building. Passing that for a moment, as meriting a separate description we come next to the White Hall. This building in architecture, material and construction is the exact counterpart of Morrill Hall. The cost of each was about $75,000, White Hall having cost somewhat the more. Having been called for some time simply the North Building its name was changed to White Hall, in honor of ex-President White, at the time when Morrill Hall received its name. The south hall of the building is entirely occupied with lecture rooms, and professors' private rooms, as is the north hall, except that the entomological laboratory occupies the entire second floor. The laboratory is fitted up with large cases which contain the specimens of the entomological museum, many thousands in number, illustrating almost every form of insect life, and collected from all parts of the world.

On the right of the middle entrance to White Hall, is Association Hall, which was furnished by President White to be used jointly by the Literary Societies and the University Christian Association. The walls of the room are decorated with nine full length bronze statuettes, made in Paris. They represent Washington, Franklin,

Shakespeare, Newton, Beethoven, Goethe, Cervantes, Dante, and Michael Angelo. Twenty large engravings, many of them proof impressions, representing interesting historical scenes are interspersed among the bronzes. The room is carpeted, comfortably seated, and well adapted for its purposes.

XIX.

Between White Hall and Morrill Hall stands the McGraw Building, so named in honor of John McGraw, who erected the building at a cost of over $120,000 and gave the same to the University. The material is the same as that of the adjoining buildings, and while differing in design, it is so constructed as to complete the symmetry of the row. The building is constructed with a main central portion, with north and south wings, the entire length of the building being two hundred and twenty feet, and its width sixty feet. A tower twenty feet square and one hundred and thirty feet high adjoins it on the west.

The middle entrance on the east side conducts the visitor by means of a double winding staircase to the second floor, which contains the main museum of the University. Just at the foot of these stairs are two immense specimens of ore, the larger, a very pure ore of copper, weighing several tons. The museum is arranged in galleries occupying the space of three floors, with a large rectangular open space in the middle. On entering the museum the first object to strike the attention is a huge plaster cast of a megatherium. On the wall over the entrance is a cast of a plesiosaurus. In the same group are casts and models of many other old monsters, "whose names are as ugly as their skeletons."

Cases around the room contain interesting archaeological collections, especially rich in both South and North American antiquities, the Trenton collection of trilobites and other fossil forms, besides a large number of skeletons, stuffed specimens and alcoholic specimens illustrative of general zoology and physiology. One of the most curious objects in the collection is a mummy of a date some eight hundred years before the Christian Era. It was secured for the University by the Hon. G. P. Pomeroy, Consul at Cairo, in 1883. The first gallery is mainly occupied by the Newcomb collection of shells, purchased by the University from Dr. Wesley Newcomb at a cost of $16,000. The collection is systematically arranged and classified, and for scientific purposes as well as for the number and beauty of the specimens is probably unequalled in the world. Cases on the east and south sides contain the collection illustrative of invertebrate life, one of the most interesting in the museum. It contains among other specimens, a fine collection of rare and beautiful corals, and a remarkable series of colored glass models of different forms of invertebrate life.

The second gallery is mostly occupied by cases containing photographs illustrative mainly of European architecture. The collection has been brought together largely by ex-President White, and contains much to interest the lover of art. From this gallery a door leads into the tower, on entering which the first object to meet the visitor is the apparatus of the University clock. There are four dial plates, one on each side of the summit of the tower, with which this mechanism is connected. It is also connected with the chime, on which it rings two notes for the first quarter, four for the second, six for the third, and eight for the fourth, striking the hour on the great bell. A narrow staircase leads up the tower to the last floor, where is located the simple apparatus by which the chime is played. A second staircase brings the visitor to the belfry. Here are hung the ten bells composing the University chime. The total weight of the chime is about 11,000 pounds, the largest bell weighing 4,889 pounds, and the smallest 230. The largest bell, the "Magna Maria," is the gift of Mrs. Andrew D. White, the other nine, composing the original chime, having been presented to the University by Mrs. Jennie McGraw-Fiske. The large bell bears the inscription, "The gift of Mary, wife of Andrew D. White, first President of the Cornell University, 1869." "Glory to God in the highest, and on earth peace, good-will toward men." "To tell of thy loving kindness early in the morning, and of thy truth in the night season;" with this stanza written expressly for it by Professor James Russell Lowell :

> I call as fly the irrevocable hours,
>   Futile as air or strong as fate, to make
> Your lives of sand or granite, awful powers ;
>   Even as men choose, they either give or take.

The nine bells, beginning with the smallest, bear the following stanzas taken from Tennyson's "In Memoriam : "

FIRST BELL.

Ring out the old, ring in the new,
Ring out the false, ring in the true.

SECOND BELL.

Ring out the grief that saps the mind ;
Ring in redress to all mankind.

THIRD BELL.

Ring out a slowly dying cause,
And ancient forms of party strife ;

FOURTH BELL.

Ring in the nobler modes of life,
With sweeter manners, purer laws.

FIFTH BELL.

Ring out false pride in place and blood ;
Ring in the common love of good.

SIXTH BELL.

Ring out the slander and the spite,
Ring in the love of truth and right.

SEVENTH BELL.

Ring out the narrowing lust of gold ;
Ring out the thousand wars of old.

EIGHTH BELL.

Ring out old shapes of foul disease,
Ring in the thousand years of peace.

NINTH BELL.

Ring in the valiant man and free,
The larger heart, the kindlier hand ;
Ring out the darkness of the land ;
Ring in the Christ that is to be.

The ninth bell bears also the following : "This
Chime the gift of Miss Jennie McGraw to the Cornell
University, 1868." The chimes are played from 7:45
to 8 A. M.; from 1 to 1:15 P. M., and from 5:45 to 6 P. M.,
on week days, and for fifteen minutes before each
chapel service on Sundays.

Descending again from the tower, and leaving the building by the main entrance, the visitor should turn to the right and enter the south wing by the door leading to the University Library. On the left of the hallway a door opens into the large Geological lecture room, fitted with maps and charts, and a fine collection of rocks and minerals for illustrative purposes. A staircase leads to the Laboratory of Geology and Paleontology, which occupies the entire second floor of this wing. On the right an entrance, protected by heavy doors of iron, gives access to the main library. This occupies a room one hundred feet long by fifty wide, and twenty feet high, filling the entire ground floor of the central portion of the building. The books are arranged in alcoves, of which there are eleven on each side of the room. The central space is occupied partly by rows of tables and chairs for readers, and partly by cases in which rare books and manuscripts are exhibited.

The Library at present consists of about sixty thousand volumes, and sixteen thousand pamphlets. It was started in 1868 by the purchase in Europe of some five thousand volumes. To this have since been added a number of private libraries, including the Goldwin Smith Historical Library, presented to the University in 1869, and a collection of Russian Folklore, presented by the Hon. Eugene Schuyler, in 1884. Between three and five thousand volumes are added every year by purchase.

The library contains not a few treasures in the way of rare and beautiful specimens of the book-makers' art. Among them are a government copy of the Napoleon work on Egypt ; a complete series of the French "Moniteur" from 1789; a set of the London "Times," beginning with the year 1848, and a set of Piranesi's engravings of Roman antiquities and works of art, the copy presented by Pope Clement, XIV., to the English Duke of Cumberland. The cases in the middle, well repay examination. One contains a collection of incunabula, or cradle collection, comprising works printed before 1500. Many of the books are adorned with beautifully illuminated initials, and some are printed on vellum. The presses of Gutemberg, Zell, Caxton, Wynkyn de Worde, and many others, are represented. There are besides a number of black letter volumes, specimens of early American printing, a book of autographs of Washington, Franklin and Lafayette, secured by the University at an expense of $1000, books with autographs from the private libraries of Leigh Hunt, Daniel Webster, Rufus Choate and others, and books illustrated by the wood-cuts of Albrecht Durer and Holbein, with other specimens of early engraving. In other cases are several Japanese and Chinese books, some costly works printed in colors, specimens of the bindings of famous craftsmen, Sanscrit, Persian, Arabic, Hindustani and Ethiopic manuscripts, several Latin manuscripts on vellum, an unpublished German passion play of the fifteenth century, a collection of French Revolutionary money, together with the autographs of most of the Presidents of the United States. On the walls of the Library are a number of paintings, among them being portraits of Mr. Cornell and Mr. McGraw, of Goldwin Smith, George William

Curtis, James Russell Lowell, and Louis Agassiz, who
are, or have been, connected with the University, either
as professors or lecturers; and of Gerrit Smith, Pru-
dence Crandall and Peter Cooper. Brackets along the
alcoves support a number of busts, representing among
others, Abraham Lincoln and President White. Ban-
ners, pennants, and other trophies of Cornell's victories
on the water and in other athletic contests, are suspended on all sides, while the cases support the various
cups and other silver emblems won in a similar manner.
In the north end of the Library a door opens into a
hallway leading to the Senior Reading Room, passing
the rooms of the Librarian on the right, and the cata-
loguing room on the left. In the west end of the Senior
Reading Room is a plaster cast of the heroic statue of
Augustus Cæsar that was unearthed in Rome some
years ago, creating a great sensation at the time. The
cast was left as a memorial by the class of 1885. A
portrait of Professor W. D. Wilson, a memorial from
the class of 1883, and one of Professor C. C. Shackford,
a memorial of the class of 1884, adorn the walls. Above
the reading room is the Anatomical Lecture Room, below
is the Anatomical Laboratory. The visitor may leave
the building by the entrance to the north wing, but
before passing on should not fail to note the handsome
drinking fountain directly in front of the middle entrance. The fountain is made of Scotch granite and
Italian marble, and cost four hundred dollars. It was
placed as a memorial by the class of 1873.

XX.

THE PHYSICAL AND CHEMICAL BUILDING.

Following the stone walk, which leads past the McGraw Building and White Hall, northward, the visitor is brought to the Physical and Chemical building, a handsome structure of red sandstone, adorned with medallions of distinguished scientists. The building was first opened for occupancy in September 1883, and cost about $85,000. It is one hundred and forty feet in length, with a width of fifty and seventy feet, and is three stories high above a well-lighted basement. To one who is interested in the sciences to which the building is devoted, it presents attractions deserving of careful study, of which no adequate description could here be given, while to the ordinary observer the varied apparatus by which the forces of nature are held in submission within its walls seems little less than magical. Entering by the main entrance, a door immediately to the right gives access to a laboratory in the basement, which contains besides a large collection of electrical apparatus, a great dividing engine, the cost of which was about $1800. It is one of the finest ever made, and is capable of ruling perfect lines on glass 30,000 or more to the inch, so fine as to be entirely invisible to the naked eye. In the rear of the laboratory are reservoirs of oxygen, hydrogen compressed air, etc., connected by pipes with various parts of the building.

From the entrance a short flight of stairs gives access
to the first floor, and a door to the right leads into the
physical lecture room. This is a large room, with seats
arranged in the form of an amphitheatre, capable of
seating about one hundred and eighty students. The
lecturer's desk is furnished with a solid pier for delicate
experiments, with electrical connections by which any
force of current can be instantly turned on, with stop-
cocks controlling supplies of oxygen and hydrogen, as
well as blast and vacuum, a small turbine for running
light machinery for experiments, and a handle connected
with a water motor which raises heavy wooden shutters
to darken the room for various purposes. A more perfect equipment could hardly be imagined. The rooms
to the rear of the lecture room and on the west side of
the hall are occupied by the Physical Laboratory,
and contain a great variety of interesting and valuable
physical apparatus. The second floor of the building
is occupied by the department of chemistry and miner-
alogy. The room for blowpiping is on the west, fitted
with tables covered with glazed porcelain, and a fine
student's collection of minerals. The chemical lecture
room is next east, similar in construction and convenience of arrangement to the physical lecture room.
From this room doors lead into the main hall, across
which another hallway leads to the eastern end of the
building to the mineralogical museum. Visitors not
unfrequently fail to see this, not knowing where it is
located. The museum contains the Silliman collection
of minerals, and is rich in rare and beautiful specimens,

which are arranged in handsome glass cases in most convenient form for exhibition. Part of the collection, including specimens of gold, silver, and diamonds, is kept in a safe in another building. The third floor of the building is entirely occupied by the chemical laboratories and the private rooms of professors. The room for qualitative practice occupying the north side, has accommodations for one hundred students. The laboratory for quantitative practice is on the east end of the building, and has places for seventy students. Each place is provided with gas, reservoir and distilled water, and suction for filtration, supplied by the air pump in the basement. Oxygen, hydrogen and blast are supplied in both rooms. There are besides, rooms for special experiments, a photographic laboratory and weighing rooms. The rooms for assaying are in the north end of the basement, and are completely equipped with furnaces, crucibles, etc.

The entire building is ventilated by a large fan in the basement, connected by flues with most of the rooms. Electricity is generated by dynamos in the basement, the power for this as well as for driving some light machinery being furnished from Sibley College by an underground connection. On the rear of the main building a long one-story brick building has just been erected to be used as a laboratory for students in applied chemistry, where the practical operations of chemical manufacture will be illustrated.

XXI.

SIBLEY COLLEGE.

East of the Physical and Chemical building stands Sibley College, facing south, and forming the northern boundary to the Campus proper. The main part is similar in material and style of construction to the three main University buildings, and is one hundred and sixty feet long, forty feet wide and three stories high. Brick workshops enclose the three remaining sides of a quadrangle of which the main building forms the front. The college with its equipment is the gift of the Hon. Hiram Sibley of Rochester, New York. The first building was erected in 1871, and in 1885 extensive additions, including the large workshops and an extension, were made, while at the same time the equipment was materially increased and the organization changed, so that to-day Sibley College ranks easily among the first of the technical schools of the country. The visitor to the college should enter by the east door, which leads him into a spacious hall, where a directory to the entire building is placed. A door on the right opens into a large lecture room, handsomely fitted with improved chairs with writing shelves attached for note-taking, and with a fine selection of models and drawings of various machines for purposes of illustration. From the main hall a stairway leads to the second story, which contains another lecture room similar to the other, adjoining which is the private room of the Director. On

the west are the various drawing rooms, and the third
floor is also occupied with drawing rooms, and the
private rooms of the instructors. On the left of the
main hall a door opens into the rooms containing
the museums and collections of the departments. The
one first entered, the east museum, contains princi-
pally a large number of samples of machines, made by
the best makers, and many of them sectioned to show
the precise manner of working. Passing through this,
and crossing a narrow hall, the visitor enters the west
museum, in the cases of which are exhibited the
Schroeder models, illustrating the forms and proportions
of various parts of machinery, and the construction of
different machines. The museum also contains the
Reuleaux collection of kinematic models, which is sup-
posed to be the only complete collection on this conti-
nent. A case on the east wall contains some interesting specimens of wood work done by students of
the college. At the north side of the museum a door
leads into a small annex, in which is located the dyna-
mo that runs the University electric light system. A
door on the left leads to the court and a few steps bring
the visitor to the foundry, equipped with an improved
Collian's cupola, and all the usual foundry appliances.
Beyond this is the smithy, which contains ten forges of
the most improved pattern. In a case on the wall
are some very interesting specimens of ornamental
forging executed by the instructor and students in this
department.

Adjoining the foundry on the east is the machine

shop, equipped with lathes, planers, grinding, drilling, and milling machines, etc. Power is supplied from a turbine located at the bottom of the gorge on the north, two hundred feet below, the connection being by means of an endless cable. Next to the machine shop is the wood-working shop, of the same size and equally well equipped. Adjoining this is the mechanical laboratory, occupying the north-east corner. This is equipped with a variety of instruments of precision adapted for making every sort of test that the engineer is called upon to secure in the course of his practice. Passing through this, the visitor enters the modelling room, in which interesting specimens of modelling in clay by students are usually to be seen. Rooms for the University Press, and apartments for the janitor occupy the remainder of the building. The circuit of the shops is now complete, and one of the most interesting parts of the institution that provides "instruction in any study" has demonstrated how thoroughly the University is fulfilling its purposes.

After leaving Sibley College no visitor should fail to cross the road on the north and follow the walk along Fall Creek gorge eastward to Triphammer Fall. Just before reaching the fall a jutting rock gives one of the finest views of the ravine anywhere to be obtained. A little beyond Triphammer Fall there is a pleasant grove on the bank that is a favorite resort of picnic parties.

XXII.

THE ENGINEERING BUILDING, AND EAST SIDE OF CAMPUS.

Adjoining the Sibley College on the east is a cottage owned by the University, next to which is a small unpretentious structure in the country school-house style. This is known in the vernacular as the "copper house," for the reason that no iron is used in its construction. In it are placed the magnetometers, and instruments for accurate electrical measurements, among which is the mammoth tangent galvanometer, constructed at the University, having coils more than six feet in diameter. From this building a road passes south on the east side of the Campus, past an orchard of some extent, to a large wooden building, at present occupied by the Engineering Department. The building was one of the first erected, and having been intended to serve temporary ends only, does not present any special merits of construction. The building contains a number of lecture and draughting rooms, private rooms for the professors of engineering, laboratories and museums. The latter contain a large collection of engineering models, and a complete collection of instruments of precision used in this profession, such as an astronomical transit, astronomical clocks, sextants, equatorials, a geodesic collection, and all the coarser field instruments. There is also a room for meteorological observations, fitted with self registering instruments. The observations

are taken daily, and the weather predictions indicated by a code of signals from the University signal
station. A temporary astronomical observatory has
been erected in the rear of the building. A portion of
the south wing is now occupied by the department of
Veterinary Science, which is soon to be transferred to a
new building erected for its especial use.

In front of the Engineering Building is the base ball
ground, the scene of many an exciting contest, and the
windows of the building are a favorite resort for those
desiring a safe vantage ground from which to witness
the contests on the diamond.

Before leaving the Campus, most visitors will be
interested in visiting the farm buildings. These are
reached by following a walk which leads directly back
of the Engineering Building to East Avenue whence a
road turns to the left leading directly to the main barn.
On the right of the road just before it reaches the barn
is a model dairy house, fitted with the most approved
appliances for managing the products of the dairy.
The barn itself is a large structure, a model of what a
barn should be. To the south and east of the barn ex-
tend the broad acres of the University Farm, on whose
green slopes pasture cattle of the choicest breeds. Just
north of the barn is the reservoir which furnishes an
ample supply of water to the Campus and buildings.
The water is pumped into the reservoir from the Fall
Creek by automatic machinery. The view from its
banks is one of the finest to be obtained from any point
on the University grounds.

XXIII.

FINAL WORD.

We have now gone somewhat in detail through the description of the University, deeming that such a description of the great State University of the Empire State might be both interesting and valuable. There is more left unsaid than has been said, but that was inevitable. We have not deemed it wise to enter upon any description of the workings of the University, or any discussion of its methods. Persons desiring such information are referred to the University Register, which is sent free to anyone on application.

Founded so wisely and so nobly, guided through the perils of its early days by so wise a hand, Cornell seems to-day to be entering upon a period of steady prosperity and internal development. Since the inauguration of President Adams many beneficial changes have been made and the promises for the future are all bright. As the sun lights her Campus by day, and the electric arcs shed their brilliant rays over her paths by night, so Cornell University stands in the realm of knowledge, adding to the light, and scattering the darkness.

XXIV.

THE GORGES.

FALL CREEK RAVINE.

To an ardent lover of the picturesque in nature, the neighborhood of Ithaca supplies an almost inexhaustible fund of keen enjoyment. The lake and town lie in a depression in the midst of a rolling plateau ; the streams that take their rise in the surrounding territory flow quietly until they reach the valley's edge, whence in a short space they descend four or five hundred feet to the level of the lake, through a series of remarkable glens or gorges abounding in deep pools, silvery cascades, and sylvan glades. Within a radius of twelve miles from Ithaca there are no less than thirty of these ravines, containing upwards of one hundred and fifty cascades, each of a beauty peculiar to itself.

The most accessible and most frequented of the glens is the Ithaca Gorge—pre-eminently " *The Gorge.*" It is indisputably the most beautiful of them all. The visitor may, for a moment, be overwhelmed by the mighty leap of the Taughannock Fall, or carried away in admiration for the grand cascade of Enfield, but he will always revert to the beauties of Fall Creek with the feeling that it, after all is most satisfactory.

The ravine lies about three-fourths of a mile to the north-east of the centre of the village and forms the northern boundary of the University premises. The

ITHACA FALL—FALL CREEK.

Fall Creek which tears its way between the precipitous walls of this defile does not, as do most of the streams of the region, pour its waters into the sluggish Inlet, but after taking its last mighty plunge over the brink of the Ithaca Fall, it winds in a tranquil, romantic course through the leafy groves of the plain directly into the lake.

It scarcely would be possible in the length of a mile to enclose by rocky walls a greater variety of beauty and grandeur. A traveller who visited the gorge in 1820, says enthusiastically, "In the rocky substance of the highest part of the mountain a dismal gulf gaps dark and wide, and far within the shaggy cliff, steep after steep in six successive leaps, Fall River rolls its current downward to the plain. This is a tremendous scene which those who have had opportunity of comparing with other remarkable places assert to be superior to all of them in the sublimest touches of nature."

To reach the gorge it is necessary only to follow out Aurora street to the north. From the bridge by which the Auburn road crosses the creek is caught the first glimpse of the finest cascade of all, the Ithaca Fall. Next to Niagara, which it nearly equals in height, it is the largest cataract in the state. It surpasses in every respect the Trenton Falls, and the cascades of the Genesee. Taughannock is higher, but for a great portion of the year its channel is nearly dry.

Formerly it was almost impossible for the most daring climber to penetrate the gorge without rope and ladder, and the visitor had to rest content with viewing the "grandeur stored within the rocky battlements" from the dizzy edges. About twenty years ago a secure pathway was hewn from the rocks along the northern wall. This path is entered through a toll gate just beyond the bridge. The ascent is at first steep and tortuous; a sharp turn or two brings the visitor to a shady nook, "The Rest," from which the glory of the grand amphitheatre about and beneath him is disclosed. This colossal basin is enclosed by steeply sloping walls more than two hundred and fifty feet in height. The slopes are draped with verdure and the crests crowned with nodding trees. The grandest feature of the view is the Ithaca Fall itself lying directly in front. The reft in the side of the amphitheatre by which the water enters seems choked by a mammoth rock eighty-five feet across at the top, which, when dry, gives the impression that a cascade of molten mineral had been suddenly hardened. The water, after flowing smoothly for some distance between lofty parallel cliffs, reaches the edge of this massive rock and plunges down the surface a hundred and fifty-six feet into the deep pool below. If the volume of water is great it is broken and beaten into a mass of seething foam, deafening in its thunder. When the water is low it trickles down in sparkling drops from shelf to shelf, festooning the brown rock with a veil of silvery spray.

From "The Rest" the walk winds midway between the pool and the summit around the semi-circular walls, to a small plateau inclining toward the very brink of the fall. Every point of this pathway affords magnificent profiles of the cataract. From this place, the path winds back and forth on the naked face of the vertical cliff, by steep ascents and dangerous looking stone stairways to the summit of the "Palisades." During the hewing out of these steps, one of the workmen accidently fell, yet without injury, nearly a hundred and fifty feet, bounding from crag to crag to the depths below. This event gained for the place the name of "Johnson's Tumble." The path leads along the edge of this precipice, known as the "Palisades" from the resemblance to the cliffs of that name on the Hudson. The dark water a hundred and twenty feet beneath, flows placidly along in the shadows of the unscalable cliffs. The perpendicular rock walls on both sides are seamed by vertical fissures which give the appearance of some immense ruined castle. From the north wall jut out two crags nearly split off, apparently ready to topple and fall crashing below. On one of these a rusty pine stands like a sentinel, grasping the rocks with its talon-like roots as in terrified desperation. Beneath, fifty yards from the edge of the fall a dam turns the water into the black mouth of the tunnel, yawning at the foot of the columnar rocks opposite. This passage through the rock conveys the water power to the mills. Formerly and for many years the water was carried to the factories by a sluice way partly hewn into the wall. Traces of this conduit may still be seen. In 1830, Ezra Cornell, then in the employ of J. S. Beebe, owner of the mill at the foot of the ravine, undertook to excavate the present tunnel. With the aid of five men he accomplished the task in about six months. From this point, may be caught glimpses of the red-tiled roof and turrets of the stately McGraw-Fiske mansion peeping through the piney fringe of the castellated cliffs across the chasm.

Passing through a grove the walk extends downward around the curve of a second amphitheatre, sometimes known as "Trouble Bay," to a little plateau directly above the second, or "Forest Fall," sixty feet in height, appropriately named from the densely wooded sides of the ravine. No word short of "magnificent" could characterize the view to the westward from this point. The deep green of the cedar-clad slopes of the foreground, the creamy foam of the fall beneath, the vertical cliffs of the "Palisades" almost meeting above the water, to make a great tube through which glorious vistas of the plains, the lake, and the hills beyond are obtained, fill one with a feeling little short of awe.

The path now takes an upward bend and soon brings to view the third fall. This, although only thirty feet high, is very beautiful. The brink is shaped rudely like the letter V ; the water rushing toward the point and falling inwards toward the narrow re-entrant angle, is beaten into a boiling froth and justifies the title of "Foaming Fall." The steep banks are still clothed with a dense growth of cedars and hemlocks and crowned with groves of deciduous tree.

Between the "Foaming Fall" and the fourth, or "Rocky Fall," the creek rushes along in a tumultuous torrent. The water at the latter cascade pours down fifty-five feet into a third amphitheatre bending towards the south. At this fall is the turbine which supplies the

THE MCGRAW-FISKE MANSION.

motive force to the University machine shops on the edge of the woody precipice two hundred feet above. Over the stream a little above the brink of the fall a swinging foot bridge is suspended on wires and connects with an interminable flight of wooden steps leading up the south side of the ravine to the University. From the bridge to the upper entrance of the gorge the creek quietly winds its romantic way under the shade of beetling cliffs and leafy bowers, and receives the name of "Sylvan Stream." The path is nearly at the water's level and follows parallel to the margin through grassy beds and forest shades.

As the head of the glen is approached the overhanging cliffs again close in, then sweep around in another great amphitheatre. The south wall is smooth and vertical; and from its crest here and there over-reaching crags project out above the abyss and afford unsurpassed points of observation.

Through a narrow passage at the head of this "Coliseum," the entire waters of the stream pour over a shelf of rock in one unbroken fall, thirty-five feet in height. The gracefully curved walls of the amphitheatre reflect and redouble the thunderous rumble of the cascade until it becomes deafening. A heavy beating as of a mighty pulse, clearly distinguishable in the midst of the uproar, gives the cataract the name of "Triphammer Fall."

From the bed of the creek a spiral staircase leads to the bank above. Until recently a bridge spanned the chasm over the crest of the fall. Above the Triphammer, the gorge narrows to a few yards. Through it the water descends from the level surface of the ground above over a dam and down a series of cascades, in whose irregular rock-floors a number of remarkable pot-holes have been worn. The path to the University along the southern brink affords many fine views. The edges of the precipice for the entire length of the gorge are fringed with shaggy groves. The volume of water in the stream never fails, and whenever the sun shines into its profound depths, the abyss is spanned by innumerable iris arches.

TRIPHAMMER FALL.--FALL CREEK.

XXV.

CASCADILLA AND SIX MILE CREEK.

After bursting from a wild, deep glen, which marks
the southern boundary of the University Grounds, the
Cascadilla Creek ripples through the village between
willow fringed banks with a cheerful murmur, little sug-
gestive of the lashings it has received in its downward
rush from the eastern hills. The Cascadilla Gorge from
the "Giant's Staircase" to where it opens into the plain,
is a series of tremendous oblong amphitheatres, whose
buttressed walls are festooned and richly decorated with
dense masses of green. There are no large falls in this
glen, but the bed of the stream is formed, to a great extent of broad plates of rock, and the water merrily
bounding from one ledge to another makes an almost
continuous series of little cascades and justifies the poetic
name of "Cascadilla. The "Giant's Staircase," the
most important of these cascades, derives its name from
the massive steps of rock over which the water tumbles
forty-five feet, in a flood of spray. The iron bridge by
which the roadway to the University crosses the gorge
spans the ravine directly above this fall. The bridge
furnishes the finest point of observation along the ravine.* The beauty and grandeur of the views obtained
from the giddy pathway leading from the village along

*See p. 41.

the edge of the precipice on the northern edge to the bridge is greatly marred by the mills, sheds, dams and rubbish heaps which do anything but add attractiveness.

Above the bridge there is a sudden change in the character of the ravine. It is no longer a gorge with awful steeps, but a sylvan glade. The stream is no longer furiously dashed into foam, but it purls along over its moss-grown bed with a cherry song, through a thicket of trees whose branches meeting over the shining water in a leafy archway, shut out the fierce beams of the sun, and make the spot one of soft and gentle loveliness.

The most important tributary to the Inlet Creek is the Six Mile Creek, which descending from the hills through a long, low ravine, circles around the base of South Hill and the southern part of the village. In the town it is shallow and broad, and during freshets and the icy season has often overflowed its banks causing considerable damage to neighboring property.

In comparison with the other streams Six Mile Creek possesses few attractions to the lover of the sublime, yet is by no means destitute of beauty. Long reaches of rather commonplace scenery (for Ithaca) by contrast enhance the beauty of the several points of interest which are unfolded at intervals. The beauty and grace of the glen is best seen by following up the bed of the channel at rather low water. High water would make it inaccessible. Along the lower part of the course much of the attractiveness has been destroyed by cutting away the trees leaving only the ugly stumps. A half mile or more from the Aurora street bridge just below a none too picturesque mill, the water plunges in two leaps of twenty feet each over exceedingly irregular moss-grown ledges into a mammoth pot-hole from which the cascade takes the name of "Well Falls." The tree-clad walls of the amphitheatre into which the stream pours, rise a hundred feet in a symmetrical curve. For three-fourths of a mile above the mill dam the rivulet winds and twists about in a serpentine course under the shade of a superb grove.

The "Narrows" is a savage chasm whose nearly ver-tical walls, eighty-five feet in height, resemble tiers of well-laid masonry. The wildness of the place is softened by a few trees growing from the pavement. Between this glen and the "Green Tree Fall," high banks shaggy with brushwood and trees confine the channel. The "Green Tree Fall," twenty-five feet in height, is re-markable for its curious formation. The sharp, ragged rocks down which the water splashes in sparkling spray, present the appearance of having once been a row of great pot-holes that had been cut vertically across the stream, and the lower part torn away. The cliffs about the fall are over sixty feet high. Above the fall the water ripples through a wild ravine containing the usual variety of miniature cascades, shaded pools and water-worn rocks. Above this, the creek wan-ders through broad cultivated fields. "High Fall," is a rarely visited cascade of sixty-five feet, on a small tributary of Six Mile Creek, ten miles from Ithaca.

XXVI.

While it is generally agreed that the Fall Creek Gorge far surpasses all others in the extent of the grandeur, beauty, and variety of its scenery, there is a great difference of opinion as to which should occupy the second place. Among the contestants for this fair honor is Buttermilk Ravine. A trip to this romantic glen is best made by going two miles down the Newfield Valley on the level road leading out from Cayuga street, and winding along the base of South Hill until the gorge is reached, and returning by the road which crosses a small bridge spanning the upper end of the ravine.

The yawning mouth of the gorge down from whose dark depths a mountain torrent comes rushing, bursts suddenly upon the view. Follow up a path a few rods along the south side of the bed of the creek, past the remains of an old saw mill, to the foot of the first and grandest fall. From the whiteness of the foaming water it is aptly named "Buttermilk Fall." The sloping face of the rock down which the glistening foam descends, is a moderately steep flight of shaly stairs overgrown with green moss and gray lichens, and honeycombed with pot-holes. Its crest is a hundred feet above the plain, and the slope, easy of ascent to the average climber, measures three hundred and fifty feet. A little way back from the brink of this great fall, the water is whipped into spray down the ragged slope of a second cascade ninety feet high, somewhat steeper, but presenting no great obstacle to the scaler. A short distance back from the top of this cascade, rises the lofty wall of the dam which collects the water for supplying the village water works, two miles away. Here the gulf widens out and rugged cliffs tower up on each side and curve around in a monstrous bowl. Out from a dismal cleft right in front, the water comes trickling down, a lace-like fringe, draping the front of a semi-circular, bulging rock which seems to choke the mouth of the cavernous defile. By some stretch of the imaginations this has been thought to resemble a pulpit, and accordingly received the name of "Pulpit Rock." This rock, the central object of interest in the gorge, may be reached by clambering up the hillside from the plateau, on the south margin, just at the point of the dam, and some rods further on descending a break-neck path into the narrow, glen, and carefully picking the way toward the front along a dangerous ledge of shale. The narrow, flume-like passage is one of the most weirdly fantastic spots of the region. The water has worn innumerable pot-holes and carved tracery on the dark walls ; the rocky overhanging crags seem almost to meet overhead ; the green roof-curtain of interlacing branches stretched across seventy feet above forbids the entrance of the sunbeams, and makes a refreshing coolness. Just above a sharp turn in this natural tunnel, and nearly at its head, is a perpendicular fall of twenty feet, whose full rich tones are re-echoed and varied by the sounding boards of rock. From this place at low water, the entire length of the creek may be traversed along its bed. Standing on the top of the last-mentioned fall, and looking up the stream, an exquisite series of six picturesque cascades, one above the other, is seen splashing in the sunlight. Their aggregate height is sixty feet. Two others of eight feet each, are just out of sight around a little turn. Pot-holes and water worn rocks abound in profusion in the sides and floors, all of them curious, many of them beautiful.

Above these the banks are low, and the few exposed rocks look like decayed masonry. The woods come down to the water's edge, and the stream ripples serenely along under a leafy tunnel, over a pavement of level plates of stone. After an abrupt bend the banks suddenly rise more than a hundred feet above, and a rare cascade of twenty-five feet blocks the way, while the creek broadens until it nearly fills the bottom of the ravine. Just above the fall there towers a curiously bent, tapering column of stone, gray with lichens, and draped with graceful clinging vines and festooned about its base with ferns. The horizontal layers projecting here and there furnish foot-holds for a daring and skillful climber. This is known variously, as the "Chimney," the "Steeple," or as "Monument Rock." On the opposite side an incomplete companion column rises a few yards. Above these pillars are several pretty cascades, all of them accompanied by the inevitable pot-holes, of all sizes, and in all stages of formation.

Not far above these the road bridge marks the end of
Buttermilk Gorge. Beyond the bridge the creek mean-
ders tranquilly through farming lands. The road which
crosses the bridge leads back to Ithaca, along the ridge
of South Hill, by a route which furnishes magnificent
pictures of the lake and valley.

XXVII.

LICK BROOK.

Most people, even in Ithaca, know of Lick Brook only vaguely by name. This glen is the wildest and most easily-traversed of the many wonderful gorges at the head of Cayuga Lake. Its beauties are so unique and so different from those of the others as not to admit of comparison with them. No trouble undertaken to visit it would be too dear a price to pay for a sight of its unique grandeur.

Lick Brook is a small stream furrowing the west slope of South Hill, a mile and a half beyond Buttermilk. It is best reached by following out Cayuga street three miles and a half to the south until a house of an almost infinite number of gables is passed. Turn to the left down a semi-private road through the barn-yard of the many-gabled house ; the road soon divides, keep to the left fork until the Inlet Creek is reached. Tie your horse to the bushes, and cross the Inlet by a crazy foot bridge at the place where the Lick Brook flows in. Cross the railroad and walk along the north bank of the little creek close to the edge ; in a few minutes the first or "Veiled Fall" is seen gleaming white through the interstices of the screen of trees which partly conceal it. The mossy rock down which the water glides is sixty feet high, nearly vertical. An unobstructed view of the fall is obtained only from the bed of the creek.

A few rods to the north of the creek a broad, but

steep path leads up the hillside to the brink of the gorge directly above the second fall, in all respects similar to the first, save in size. From this eminence the descent to the channel of the brook is gentle. The view looking up the ravine contains nothing of the majestic ; it is a charming vista of loveliness. The mossy velvet of the banks is covered with masses of feathery fern and delicate wild flowers. The sunlight sifting down through the intertwining leaves far above, dispels all gloominess. The coolness throughout the glen, even on the hottest days, is delicious. Walk up the delightful hollow over the shale ledges of the miniature cascades, and you come suddenly upon a wonderful crevice fissuring the south wall. The rocks nearly meet fifty feet overhead. Its stony bottom slopes inward and upward at a sharp angle for seventy feet. Eagle Cavern is the name given to it. Just beyond this tremendous cleft the walls suddenly rise to a height of a hundred and sixty feet, and bend away in the form of a mighty amphitheatre. The sides slope backward for eighty feet, then rise perpendicularly for eighty feet more. The incline is carpeted with delicate forest plants, and magnificent forest trees rise in tiers wherever they can gain a precarious hold. The glen again narrows and bends around at a right angle ; the dark gray shaded rocks over whose shelves the water descends in a series of little falls give the name of Dark Cascade. Savage cliffs overhang the well-like amphitheatre into which the passage of the Dark Cascade opens. Around another sharp corner, over a gently sloping floor, as regularly seamed and jointed as a pavement, lies the way to the final and grandest scene of all.

The narrow entrance to this stupendous, chamber is
guarded by two funnel-shaped pillars, one on either
side. Once past the rocky portal, and an exclamation
of astonishment cannot be repressed. You are in
a tremendous oblong bowl, entirely surrounded save
for the crevice through which admission is gained.
The curved rock walls are vertical and overhang. At
its remotest end a strange rock formation leans against
the smooth wall of the perpendicular cliff. This has
been compared to the half of a haystack. Directly
above this the water of the creek comes rushing down
a short inclined and moss-lined channel, takes a head-
long leap clear of the brink, and is dashed in spray
on the conical rock a hundred and forty feet below. The gray and lofty walls ; the massy columns at
the door ; the overhanging roof a hundred and sixty
feet above ; the azure canopy; the eastward altar, hung
with its adornments of velvet moss ; the richly blending
colors ; the profound peace, broken only by the sweet,
solemn chant of the mist-robed choir, mingled with the
deep-toned accompaniment of the wind-swept evergreens
fringing the crests, make the grandeur of the scene sol-
emnly impressive. No name could be more appropriate
than "The Cathedral."

If the visitor has come thus far, he will not need to
be told to turn around and go back. The vertical cliffs
surrounding him do not offer the faintest suggestion of
any passage over them. It is possible, of course, to go
back and follow up the ravine on the bank ; but having
shown you its grand cathedral, Lick Brook has given
you its best.

LUCIFER FALL--ENFIELD.

XXVIII.

Next to the Fall Creek Gorge, the Enfield Glen is most frequented by visitors. It is inferior in many respects to the former, whose wonders it repeats with variation. The head of the gorge is between six and seven miles from Ithaca, and is reached by driving out, either on Cayuga street, or along the street at the foot of West Hill, for both roads unite three miles from town. A guide-board at a division of the road, just before reaching the house of many gables, points to the right-hand fork. Follow this past a little bridge, and up the hill for two miles. Just beyond a white school-house, turn to the left down a steep pitch into the little village of Enfield Falls. The small, neatly kept hotel down a green lane to the left, will provide you with a dinner or lunch, upon which the most fastidious could not fail to pass emphatic approval. The entrance to the gorge lies at the end of a path leading from the hotel. The expense of keeping the road through the glen in order is defrayed by a toll of ten cents on each visitor. The beautiful valley from which the ravine opens, was evidently the bed of an ancient lake. The creek cuts squarely through the hill by a narrow cleft, the portal of which is flanked by massive door posts of rock. The angular joints and horizontal strata confirm the impression that the long passage-way had been hewn out and walled up by skillful masons of ages ago. The shelving

layers of harder rock make an excellent flooring for the
pathway. A short distance within the defile in the cliff
on the right, is a small chamber curiously hollowed out
by nature to resemble a huge old-fashioned square fire-
place, capable of concealing a half dozen people within
its cavernous recess. The water twelve feet below you
rippling over the low ledges makes a number of pretty
little cascades, whirls around eddying pools in the
curious pot-holes, and at last enters a wonderful flume,
long, deep, straight and smooth, not more than twenty
inches in width, down which it shoots with arrow swift-
ness. Twenty feet above this strange channel a bridge
spans the gorge, and for the remainder of the distance
the path follows the left margin of the stream. A sharp
turn and a steep descent bring you into a great basin
in whose bottom has been hollowed a mammoth pot-
hole, the Bath-tub of Lucifer, to which the boiling water
is brought by the conduit above mentioned. The walls
of this amphitheatre are fissured, and partly covered by
scanty bushes and stunted trees.

Another turn and another descent bring you to the
brink of a noble flight of rocky stairs down whose ledges
the water tumbles in a mass of frothy whiteness into a
second grand chamber. The level floor of this vast
room is one great sheet of rock, surrounded by vertical
walls towering sublimely a hundred feet. This square
saloon was thought by some imaginative person to be
worthy of the uses of His Satanic Majesty and was accordingly named "Lucifer's Kitchen."

From this Mephistophelian bake house follow the
narrow path around the base of a majestic promontory

which conceals the grandeur yet to be disclosed, and
you suddenly shrink back in amazement at the sight
before you. You are on the very brink of a mighty
precipice over which the creek pours its waters to break
in foam on jutting rocks, and finally to take a final
desperate plunge into a great basin a hundred and forty
feet below. This is Lucifer Fall. Whether dyspepsia
or theology is to blame for the satanic names attached
to the most interesting points in Enfield Ravine is a
point that is not quite clear. From the brink of the
fall the path descends by a flight of wooden steps, hugs
the face of the cliff for a way and then crosses a rickety
bridge to a jutting buttress that commands a fine view
of the fall. You stand directly facing the first leap of
the fall and gazing down, not without a shudder, into
the abyss below. From this point the path descends
rapidly to the bottom of the ravine. Where the path
ends the stream can generally be crossed to the opposite
side, from which is obtained the most impressive view
of the entire fall. The tree crowned cliffs appear almost to meet two hundred and seventy feet above. In
front the water climbs to meet the clouds. The fall is
not one smooth leap, but is considerably broken. In
low water the fall is really four separate cascades, but
when the stream is swollen, the water comes over in
one unbroken mass, disregarding all small impediments.

This is the culmination of the scenery in Enfield Ravine. Few visitors care to go further. For two miles
below, the scenery is that of an ordinary pretty glen,
but there is no path, and one hardly feels repaid for the
rough climb in making the trip.

XXIX.

ON THE SHORES OF CAYUGA.

The fair sheet of water that bears the poetic name of Cayuga, contributes its full share toward the variety and charm of the scenery surrounding Ithaca. One of the great chain of lakes that form so striking a feature of the geography of Central New York, Seneca Lake alone ventures to dispute its title to the crown of the series. For thirty-eight miles does the lake wind its way northward from Ithaca to Cayuga Bridge, varying in width from a little over one mile to nearly four, and in some places attaining a depth of some four hundred feet. The scenery along its shores is varied and interesting. In one place perpendicular cliffs rise abruptly from the very edge of the lake. Again, smooth hills slope back in graceful undulations, adorned with pleasant country homes. At frequent intervals streams of greater or less size flow in, usually falling over several pretty cascades just at the lake's brink. Summer hotels and private cottages seem to line the banks. The Cayuga lake boats leave Ithaca at 7 a. m., reach Cayuga Bridge about 10:30 to connect with the train on the New York Central Railroad, and returning, reach Ithaca at three in the afternoon. To one in search of a day of quiet enjoyment, nothing could be suggested in everyway more satisfactory than this trip on a pleasant summer day. No matter how warm the day, the lake is always cool. The dark blue water, clear and pure, wells up from deep springs that know not summer sun. The constant change in the scenery, the bustle at the various little landings, clear sky and pure air, all combine to furnish the keenest enjoyment and gratification.

On the east shore of the lake, some three miles from Ithaca, begins a series of palisade-like cliffs, presenting a peculiar and interesting jointed formation of the rocks. No better specimen of this structure exists anywhere, and Prof. Dana in his manual of Geology has presented an illustration of these rocks to show this formation. The Cayuga Lake Railroad runs along just at the base of these cliffs. This road follows the edge of the lake for its entire length. In winter storms, the water is not infrequently blown across the track, and freezing there, makes the road impassible. Burdick's Glen, Shurger's Ravine, and the Ludlowville Gorge, all join the lake between Ithaca and Ludlowville, a distance of some seven miles. On the west bank of the lake pretty summer cottages dot the wooded banks as far as Glenwood, three miles. Glenwood occupies a little point that juts out into the lake, and is fitted up with many conveniences for the transient visitor. No one who visits it on a summer afternoon or evening, can doubt its popularity. A short distance beyond Glenwood a long narrow point runs out into the lake. This is Crowbar Point, the same that appears to shut off the view to one looking down the lake from Ithaca. Beyond this point the lake bends quite sharply to the westward. Some four miles beyond, Taughannock landing is reached, where a low peninsula has been built out some distance into the lake by the materials which the stream has brought down from the rocky hills.

About half way between Crowbar Point and Taughannock, Tower Rock stands out boldly from the shore. In structure this resembles somewhat the well-known Steeple Rock of Buttermilk ravine. At Taughannock the Tully limestone first crops out. As the dip of this stratum is toward the south, it gradually rises higher and higher above the lake as we proceed northward, and every little stream that comes into the lake takes its final plunge over this limestone ledge, whose hardness resists all erosive effects. Frequently the softer strata under the limestone have crumbled away under the action of the water, forming fantastic recesses. Some fifteen miles down the lake are Kidder's Ferry, and, a little beyond, Sheldrake, both popular summer resorts. Aurora, on the opposite side, is a charming village, the seat of Wells College and of the Cayuga Lake Military Academy. Some miles beyond Aurora is Union Springs, noted especially for its plaster. The geological structure around this village presents many points of interest to the student. The lower end of the lake at the outlet is a great marsh. In addition to the passenger traffic on the lake, which is very considerable during the season, there is a large freight traffic especially in coal, carried on by means of canal boats. The Lehigh Valley R. R. brings the coal from the Pennsylvania coal fields to Ithaca, where it is loaded in canal boats ready to be taken to any place that is reached by the great canal system of the state.

TAUGHANNOCK FALL.

XXX.

TAUGHANNOCK.

No other place on Cayuga's shores is deservedly so famous as Taughannock Fall. Poets have sung its beauty, travelers have rhapsodized over its grandeur and sublimity, and commonplace people have declared that it was very nice. It is better known as a resort than any other place in the vicinity, as it is more convenient of access from the centres of population, being on a branch of the Lehigh Valley. Travelers from a distance generally come to Taughannock by this railroad, but no visitor from Ithaca should do so. If an e rly morning start is not too grave an objection, the route by the steamboat is in every way delightful. The boat leaves the dock about 7 a. m., reaching Taughannock in about an hour. Returning it leaves the landing about 2 p. m., giving ample time for a visit to the fall. In case a congenial party can be made up, nothing is pleasanter than to charter a steam yacht for the day, as the company can then go and come at their own convenience.

Let us suppose that we start from the steamboat landing, no matter how we have arrived there. The road leads up the hill a little way, and then branches, one branch turning to the right along the lake shore, the other going straight on up the hill. Both ways are the road to Taughannock, but as we cannot go both ways at once, let us try the right hand road. This presently brings us to a bridge over the Taughannock stream, here broad and shallow. Again the question arises, shall we follow up the bed of the stream, or continue along the road. We ought to do both, and the best advice that can be given is to go twice, and whichever route you chose on your first visit, choose the other on your second. This time, however, we will continue our course along the road beyond the bridge, soon turning to the left, and ascending a steep hill. After climbing a considerable way we come at last to a pretty little rustic hotel, with pleasant grounds surrounding. The hotel stands almost on the very edge of the ravine, along the bank of which seats are placed that command a fine view of the Fall, and the amphitheatre below. Tarry here awhile, if you can, for although the distance diminishes the impressiveness of the Fall itself, the scene is none the less stately and full of beauty. But presently seek out the staircase that leads to the bottom of the ravine, and go down, down till you feel sure there are no deeper depths. Then follow up the bed of the stream, along a pathless path, till you stand in the clearing before "The Great Fall in the Woods." Round about you on either side the rock rises three hundred and fifty feet almost perpendicular. Just in front, the cliffs are broken, and the Bridal Veil of Taughannock is hung down from the cleft to cover the bare face of the rocks. The water falls in one sheer perpendicular leap two hundred and fifteen feet. At most seasons of the year it is for the most part dissipated into a silvery spray long before reaching the bottom, really only a veil through which glimpses of the cliff behind may be caught. The fall is symmetrical in outline, and possesses a regularity and perfectness not found in any of the other cascades of the region. Before leaving, come up close to the fall, no matter if it may sprinkle you a little, and stand quiet a moment till the spell of the silent water falling from its majestic height comes over you, as it surely will. The feeling is indescribable. If you please you can now retrace your steps a little way down the glen and find a pathway leading up the opposite side from that on which you descended. It is steep, arduous, and the steps are many before the top is reached. But it is worth while to make the effort to climb out on one side or the other, for otherwise some of the finest views would be missed. Let us go back this time to the little hotel whence we started, in order that our exploration may have some continuity. From the hotel we can now see more than we could before, and can better appreciate the scene. Calling on the imagination for a little aid, perhaps you will be able to make out the figure of "The Maid of the Mist," sitting pensively behind the fall, her head turned from it and bent down as though in deep thought. Beyond the hotel, we must follow the road for some little distance, occasionally turning aside to the brink of the ravine to catch the changing views, until presently a somewhat dilapidated booth with a still more dilapidated turnstile on one corner, marks for you the beginning of the path that will lead you to the bed of the creek above the fall. Although you are only going above the fall, still the descent is nearly a hundred and fifty feet, and is full of striking features. A rustic bridge crosses the stream a little way above the Fall. The view up the stream is charming, and though few visitors ascend the gorge above the main fall, the beauties of the upper ravine well repay those who do for their labor. From the bridge a path leads up the bank on the opposite side. But follow the edge of the stream for a distance, before ascending the path. Just beyond the brink of the Fall a broad shelf of rock several feet wide extends for some thirty or forty feet under the brow of the cliff. From this is disclosed the most impressive sight of all. From the shelf you cannot see the bottom of the ravine immediately in front of you, and you seem therefore to be suspended in mid-air. Right by your side the water slides quietly off the edge of the cliff, and one can hardly realize that it is taking such a tremendous plunge in so quiet a manner. Looking directly across the vast amphitheatre, you gain some adequate conception of its magnitude. From cliff to cliff in the widest part is more than six hundred feet. The views down the ravine toward the lake add their own exquisite portion to complete the majesty and beauty of the view.

You may now return to the path, and follow it through well-kept grounds, furnished with pleasant arbors and comfortable seats along the south brink of the ravine. Lookouts here and there command fine prospects of the Fall and surroundings. To the right is a half public house, where refreshment may be sought if needed. Beyond this, the path soon joins the road, which winds picturesquely down the hill giving most delightful prospects of the lake and valley at every turn. At the foot of the hill we come to the fork where we decided to go the other way, and continue to the landing with the resolve to come again soon, and make the trip the other way first.

XXXI.

MORE RAVINES STILL.

Those ravines that present the most striking features
and most often attract the notice of the tourist or pleas-
ure seeker have now been described, together with at least
one good way to reach each of them. But there are many
more that in any region less richly favored than Ithaca,
would be esteemed worthy of the most elaborate description. Such a one is Coy's Glen or the Artist's Ravine,
in the side of West Hill a mile below the Depot. It is
full of delightful nooks, and is a favorite resort for those
who seek the early blooming arbutus in the first fragrance of spring. At Ludlowville, also, the Ludlowville Falls, and the Indian Falls awaken an enthusias-
tic appreciation of their beauties in every visitor. Burdick's Glen and Shurger's Ravine on the east shore of
the lake, nearer than Ludlowville, reward the tourist
richly. At Trumansburg Landing, a mile and a half
north of Taughannock, a large stream empties into the
lake upon which are two superb falls, a hundred, and
a hundred and fifty feet in height.

At the other end of our territory, some seven miles
down the Inlet valley, the Newfield Ravine and the so-
called West Branch, afford scenes which are said to rival
anything the Lake country can present. Every little
stream conforms to the general structure of the country,
and in so doing makes itself as beautiful as it can.

XXXII

THE DRIVES.

In directing the visitor how to reach the various ravines that have been described, some of the finest of
the many fine drives about Ithaca have been incidently
touched upon. While it will not be possible to give detailed directions for guiding a horse and carriage through
the country, it may not be inappropriate to mention a
few of the drives that are the most attractive. Among
these that to Ludlowville along the lake road, well de-
serves mention. The road is simply a continuation of
Aurora street to the north, crossing Fall Creek right in
front of the great Ithaca Fall, and running along the
edge of the lake some distance, and then rising in a
slope that commands magnificent views of the lake below. The road passes through Libertyville, better
known as Rogue's Harbor, and again descends to Ludlowville. The entire distance is nearly ten miles. The
drive on the opposite side of the lake to Trumansburg
is equally beautiful and even more popular. The road
ascends the hill beyond the depots on the west of the
valley in a long, gradual slope, commanding a grand
view of the Lake almost all the way, and then runs
along the crest of the hill through an interesting country
twelve miles to Trumansburg. This is a favorite route
for sleigh-riding parties. The drives up the valley to
the south have already been dwelt upon. One of the

pleasantest drives in the region is that to Varna or Etna. The traveller should take the road that leads through the University Grounds ; thence the road leads eastward through a forest road along the brink of Fall Creek Ravine to Forest Home, a pretty little hamlet of decidedly rural aspect. Keep the right hand road, which presently crosses a bridge, and winds for some distance along the very edge of the picturesque stream. Nothing could be more delightful than this part of the drive. The scenery beyond is varied and interesting. The little village of Varna is some two miles beyond Forest Home, and Etna, a somewhat larger small place, is about four miles further.

XXXIII.

How to get into Ithaca, and how to get out again, are questions often asked, and not always easily answered. The town is peculiarly situated as regards its connections with the outside world. No great trunk line strikes it, and no less than four small railroads do. The steamboat line makes a fifth means of ingress and egress.

Ithaca can be reached by the New York Central, the Erie, the Delaware & Lackawanna, and the Lehigh Valley railroads. The traveler on the New York Central, will leave the train at Canastota, and take the Elmira, Cortland & Northern [E.C.& N.] road, if coming from the east ; if coming from the west, he should leave the Central at Lyons, and take the Geneva, Ithaca & Sayre [G.I.& S.] road, the latter being now controlled by the Lehigh Valley. The trains of the Cayuga Lake road connect with the old branch of the Central at Cayuga Bridge, making still another route. The traveler on the Erie, if from the east, will leave it at Owego, to take the Cayuga branch of the D. L. & W. If from the west, he may take the E. C. & N. at Elmira. The directions for one traveling by the D. L. and W., are similar to those for an Erie traveler. Travelers by the Lehigh Valley, change at Sayre to the G. I. & S., in the day ; at night a through sleeper leaves Jer-

sey City for Ithaca.   In Ithaca the depots of the G. I.
& S., the Cayuga Lake road, and the D. L. & W.,
are all in the extreme western part of the village, at the
foot of West Hill.   The two former roads occupy the
depot farther west together ; the latter road has the
eastern depot.   The depot of the E. C. & N. road is
on the summit of East Hill, a mile and a half from the
centre of the village.   Lines of stages run to all the
depots.   The steamboat landing is on the Inlet at the
foot of Cayuga Street.   Time tables change so that
their insertion here would be more likely to do evil than
good.   All the roads have ticket offices in the centre of
the village where full information may be obtained.